Marjorie Hillis (1889–1971) worked for *Vogue* for over twenty years, beginning her career as a captions writer for the pattern book and working her way up to assistant editor of the magazine itself. She was one of a growing number of independent, professional women who lived alone by choice. In 1936 she wrote *Live Alone and Like It*, the superlative guide for 'bachelor ladies' (who became known as 'live-aloners'). It was an instant bestseller and created a phenomenon.

Three years after the book's publication, at the age of forty-nine, Ms Hillis bid a fond farewell to the live-aloners by marrying Mr T. H. Roulston.

LIVE ALONE
AND
LIKE IT

THE ART OF SOLITARY REFINEMENT

BY MARJORIE HILLIS

with a Preface by

LISA HILTON

DRAWINGS BY CIPÉ PINELES

virago

VIRAGO

Published in Great Britain by Virago Press in 2005
This edition published by Virago Press in 2017

5 7 9 10 8 6

First published in the United States of America by
The Bobbs-Merrill Company in 1936

A CIP catalogue record for this book
is available from the British Library.

ISBN 978-1-84408-125-7

Typeset in American Garamond by M Rules
Printed and bound in Great Britain by
Clays Ltd, St Ives plc

Papers used by Virago are from well-managed forests
and other responsible sources.

MIX
Paper from
responsible sources
FSC® C104740

Virago Press
An imprint of
Little, Brown Book Group
Carmelite House
50 Victoria Embankment
London EC4Y 0DZ

An Hachette UK Company
www.hachette.co.uk

www.virago.co.uk

CONTENTS

CONTENTS – *Concluded*

PREFACE

MANUALS for the single woman have existed since the invention of the printing press, and even before. From the codes of the mediaeval convent to the encouragingly titled *Afternoon of Unmarried Life* published by an 'unmarried gentlewoman of England' in 1959, to Helen Gurley Brown's 1962 *Sex and the Single Girl* and Anna Johnson's radically millennial *Three Black Skirts: All You Need to Survive*, women have been bossed, bullied, cajoled and consoled about the pleasures and pitfalls of the single life for the best part of a thousand years. Curiously, no equivalent of what is very distinctly a genre exists for the enlightenment of men, although given the statistical commonplace that single men die younger, commit suicide more frequently, suffer more health problems and have an altogether duller time than their married counterparts, it would appear that they are sorely in need of it. Perennially, it is women who are singled out, whose solitary state, elective or not, is somehow seen as a problem to be solved. The inherent premise of any and all such manuals is that the lone woman is in need of guidance to overcome the terrors of her peculiar and undesirable solitude. Marjorie Hillis makes no bones about her subject's lack of a clear social role, firmly subtitling *Live Alone and Like It* 'a guide for the extra woman' (as was the subtitle of the original 1936 edition). Any good feminist would presumably toss all such rubbish in the dustbin and read a proper book. Yet women still buy these manuals, and women still write them, and the newspapers are still full of horrific stories about single women being responsible for nearly all the social evils working mothers can't be blamed for, and singleness in a woman, no matter how brilliant or successful she may be, is still represented as odd. That being the case, why is *Live Alone and Like It*, published in 1936 and presumably therefore entirely irrelevant to the twenty-first-century woman, worth reading?

Live Alone is a joyful reminder that feminism wasn't just about hunger strikes and bra burning. It sits roughly between the two major waves of the feminist movement, the achievement of suffrage after the First World War and women's liberation in the sixties and early seventies, and the sense of energy and power it derives from the former subtly anticipates the latter. Demure though some of the advice may be, as in the chapter on affairs entitled 'Will You or Won't You?' (which concludes, rather darkly, that 'the woman always pays') *Live Alone* is nevertheless suffused with a sense of exuberance at the thrilling possibilities then open to women for the first time. For the writer, and reader, in 1936, the single woman had been until very recently embalmed by popular imaginings in the crocheted catafalque of the 'maiden lady'. Dusty, worthy, unloved and unwanted, a woman whose inclusion in any social event was a burdensome duty, whose virtue existed by default, the fate of the old maid was so dispiriting that it was hardly surprising most women felt marriage to be a matter of social life and death. Yet when Marjorie Hillis published her book, women had thrown away their hobble skirts and taken jobs in factories and offices – they were driving cars and voting for presidents, drinking martinis and wearing lipstick, activities which seem ordinary enough now, but which then augured the debut of a truly brave new world. A feminist vocabulary is already firmly in play: living alone, the book declares, will be difficult 'if you have a dated mind and still think of yourself as belonging to the weaker sex'. Independence is freshly perceived as an exhilarating necessity, and 'anyone who pities herself for more than a month on end is a weak sister, and likely to become a public nuisance besides.' Living alone requires strength of character, the book suggests, implying that such strength is an obligation extracted in return for the first steps towards equality. However, *Live Alone* is quite clear that the achievement of such strength is a struggle, as indeed, in 1936, it still was.

Unlike her contemporary equivalents therefore, Marjorie (and after the first few pages she is definitely 'Marjorie'), is not a hypocrite. Rather, she does not have to perform an awkward juggling act between pretending that living alone is wonderful and empowering whilst essentially giving advice on how to face the dreadful fact that one has failed to get married. Marjorie admits right from the start that her book is 'no brief in favour of living alone', but an encouragement to women to make the best of 'solitary refinement', if 'only now and then between husbands'. *Live Alone and Like It* is about making the best possible virtue of necessity, which is really what all those other books are about too, though it's no longer politically correct to admit it. Cognitive dissonance dissipates with a spritz of eau de toilette, and we can get on with enjoying the advice, which is really rather good.

One of the most refreshing aspects of *Live Alone* is that it makes no mention of the dread twenty-first-century palliative – therapy. Freud had long been published by the time Marjorie was writing, but presumably she was too busy whipping up canapés and dashing off to the theatre to read him. Personal improvement, the *Live Alone* way, is not nurturing one's self-esteem like a sick puppy, but taking an honest look at one's failings of character and appearance, and doing something about them. Blaming others for one's putative loneliness, or expecting to be helped, is the first cardinal sin of the solitary woman: 'martyrdom may be an interesting role to its player, but it is a terrible bore to everyone else.' If you are bored and lonely, Marjorie suggests, blame it on your own lack of initiative. 'If you're interesting, you'll have plenty of friends, and if you're not, you won't, unless you're very, very rich.' Being interesting need not depend on income (the book includes a long list of cheap but engaging activities for the enterprising girl about New York which could easily, with a little imagination, be updated for any modern city), but it does depend on cultivation. Being well-read and well-informed, learning to listen and draw people out, taking the trouble to refine one's taste and develop one's ideas about paintings, or plays, or politics are not suggested as strategies whose primary goal is to ensnare a man, but as the duty of any sensible, intelligent human being who wishes to have a social life.

Live Alone proposes sociability as an essential requirement for the solitary woman. 'Hermits and other self-sufficient people may be geniuses', raps Marjorie briskly, 'and contribute greatly to the scientific knowledge of the world, but they contribute practically nothing to its entertainment, and have a very dull time themselves.' This suggestion is not so far from Helen Fielding's idea in her book about the famous 'singleton' Bridget Jones, that friends create an 'urban family' which can provide support and comfort in the absence of more traditional ties. Being interested and interesting seems a decent recipe for a good social life, in 1936 or now, in the twenty-first century.

Practically, *Live Alone* bases its suggestions on the

cheering thought that the lone woman may do exactly as she pleases. A solitary bathroom, Marjorie affirms, is truly one of life's great blessings. However, along with freedom comes responsibility. Environment, for instance, 'matters much more than if you had a husband or even a lover.' Chic is paramount in the single woman's ideal home, with comfort coming second, on the grounds that many people put it first, and the results are what oblige it to come second. Don't economise on flowers, and beware of the dispiriting effects of snack meals on one's morale. As for decoration, clutter, Marjorie daringly suggests, 'is as outdated as modesty'. Equally precise is the chapter on the pleasure of a single bed, most gaily illustrated with a very cheerful marcel-waved lady smoking a cigarette beneath a frilly satin quilt, wearing a slinky negligee and an alluring pout. A mirror is recommended opposite the bed so its occupant may be viewed when sitting up: 'This is sometimes depressing, but it acts as a prompter when you feel yourself slipping.' As to any other activities in the bedroom, Marjorie considers them too vulgar to mention, but there is a deliciously discreet hint about self-satisfaction on page 75.

Appearance, for the single girls' manual, is always a vexed question. Only the witless believe that women squeeze themselves into wonderbras and impossible shoes for their own benefit, yet looking dreadful has conversely never done much for anybody's confidence. Marjorie is in no doubt that clothing is the objective correlative of the psyche, and whilst bed jackets, quilted satin or otherwise, are no longer much worn, the point that one may as well have pretty things as ugly ones, even if no one is going to see them, does not seem unreasonable. The assertion that many women live alone through the wrong choice of face cream is, however, one piece of advice the modern reader could dispense with. Marjorie's recommendations as to make-up and fashion obviously need to be considered as principles, rather than models, and the same is true with her suggestions on food and entertaining. The post-modern cult of the domestic goddess can seem like one more stick to beat harassed women with, and *Live Alone*'s suggestions on entertaining on a small budget in a small space seem, surprisingly, more modern. The appeal of those 'thrown together' kitchen suppers sometimes seems like an insidious way of prodding women back to the stove; fine if you have all day to do the throwing, the money for those oh-so-simple rustic ingredients and a kitchen the size of the average flat, but otherwise as relevant to the way most women eat and entertain as a recipe by Fanny Cradock. *Live Alone* proposes plenty of good drinks, use of the delicatessen counter, and effort expended on conversation. Equal space is given to the solitary splendour of the large breakfast in bed, which is far more uplifting than mucking about with calves' liver after a hard day at the office.

Live Alone and Like It will not tell you how to have a better orgasm or marry a millionaire. Nor will it insult you by telling you that a massage will relieve your inner angst or that overdressed teenagers masquerading as women in a prime-time television show are role models through which you can know yourself better. It is stern, though witty, about the need for women to manage their money properly, and it won't pretend that your life will be revolutionised if you starve off ten pounds. In many ways, it is a dated book – it does not consider single women with children or gay women, and maids are not so easy to come by as they were in 1936. Yet it is emphatically a grown-up book, despite its playfulness, and a tremendous pleasure to read, whether or not one is in need of advice at all. In general though, Marjorie concludes, if you follow her guidance, 'you will probably not have to live alone and like it' anyway.

LISA HILTON

CHAPTER ONE

SOLITARY REFINEMENT

THIS book is no brief in favor of living alone. Five out of ten of the people who do so can't help themselves, and at least three of the others are irritatingly selfish. But the chances are that at some time in your life, possibly only now and then between husbands, you will find yourself settling down to a solitary existence.

You may do it from choice. Lots of people do — more and more every year. Most of them think that they are making a fine modern gesture and, along about the second month, frequently wish they hadn't.

1

Or you may — though, of course, you don't — belong to the great army of Lonely Hearts with nobody to love them. This is a group to which no one with any gumption need belong for more than a couple of weeks, but in which a great many people settle permanently and gloomily.

The point is that there is a technique about living alone successfully, as there is about doing anything really well. Whether you view your one-woman ménage as Doom or Adventure (and whether you are twenty-six or sixty-six), you need a plan, if you are going to make the best of it.

The best can be very nice indeed. As nice, perhaps, as any other way of living, and infinitely nicer than living with too many people (often meaning two or more others) or with the wrong single individual. You can live alone gaily, graciously, ostentatiously, dully, stolidly. Or you can just exist in sullen loneliness, feeling sorry for yourself and arousing no feeling whatever in anybody else.

Your choice in this matter need have nothing to do with your income. If it's a small one, you'll probably find more other solitary dwellers living at about your level than you would if it were large — and these odd numbers will prove to be your greatest assets as last-minute dinner-guests, fourths at bridge, and theater companions.

If you have lived alone for a long time, you will have your own scheme of living, and our words of wisdom will only give you a few scattered suggestions. But for the benefit of those who are new at this particular game of solitaire, we will start at the beginning.

The beginning is your attitude – your approach, so to speak. For the basis of successful living alone is determination to make it successful. Whether you belong to the conservative school that calls it will-power, or the modern school that calls it guts, the necessity is there. You have got to decide what kind of a life you want and then make it for yourself. You may think that you must do that anyway, but husbands and families modify the need considerably. When you live alone, practically nobody arranges practically anything for you.

This business of making your own life may sound dreary – especially if you have a dated mind and still think of yourself as belonging to the Weaker Sex. But it really isn't. You can have a grand time doing it. You can – within the limitations imposed on most of us, whether we live singly or in herds – live pretty much as you please. To be sure, you will have nobody to make a fuss over you when you are tired, but you will also have nobody to expect you to make a fuss over him, when you are tired. You will have no one to be responsible for your bills – and also no one to be responsible to for your bills. You will be able to eat what, when, and where you please, even dinner served on a tray on the living-room couch – one of the higher forms of enjoyment which the masculine mind has not yet learned to appreciate.

You can, in fact, indulge yourself unblushingly – an engaging procedure which few women alone are smart enough to follow. Being Spartan becomes pointless when there is no one to watch your performance. Even unselfishness requires an opponent – like most of the worthwhile things in life. Living alone, you can – within your own walls – do as you like. The trick is to arrange your life so that you really do like it.

It may seem difficult at first – especially if the move wasn't your idea anyway. A great many people take this step after a death, divorce, or some rearrangement of relationships that seems like a catastrophe. They are pretty sure to feel a little sorry for themselves, slightly expectant of sympathetic attention, and all too ready to have a chip on the shoulder. This is only human. Everybody feels sorry for herself (to say nothing of himself) now and then. But anyone who pities herself for more than a month on end is a weak sister and likely to become a public nuisance besides.

Of course, you don't need to do this – if you'll face a few facts. The first one is that – to put it baldly – an extra woman is a problem. Even those as alluring as Peggy Joyce (whose periods of being extra women are brief, but may be frequent). Extra women mean extra expense, extra dinner-partners, extra bridge opponents, and, all too often, extra sympathy.

This may come to you as a shock. Perhaps you have always thought that you were the belle of the neighborhood. Or perhaps you knew you weren't, but thought you had a few staunch friends and relatives. And probably you have – but even they will sometimes wonder what to do about you.

The idea is to do it yourself – and to do it first. But to do it well, you'll need at least two things: a mental picture of yourself as a gay and independent person, and spunk enough to get the picture across to the other person.

We know, for example, one business woman who forty years ago would have been described as a maiden lady and who, during the vacations, weekends, and evenings incidental to twenty years in an office, has managed to shoot in Scotland, bathe at Juan-les-Pins, cross the Andes, see the races at Saratoga, go to most of the best plays in New York, and keep her figure. 'I'm naturally lazy,' she says, 'but I get around some, because I'm *not going to be a Maiden Aunt*. I'm not going to have my married brothers and sisters, and my nieces and nephews, feel about me as I felt about my father's unmarried sister. When I was young, we couldn't so much as go for a buggy ride without wondering if we oughtn't to stop and get Aunt Mary – she went out so seldom. Well, I intend to go out just as often as anyone in my family, if not a little bit oftener. And what's more, I intend to go just a little bit farther.'

We don't know just how far she does go, but we have never heard her referred to as a Maiden Lady.

There is an element of defiance in this attitude, but when you start to live alone, defiance is not a bad quality to have handy. There will be moments when you'll need it, especially if you've been somebody's petted darling in the past. But you will soon find that independence, more truthfully than virtue, is its own reward. It gives you a grand feeling. Standing on your own feet is extraordinarily exhilarating, and being able to do very well (when it's necessary) without your friends, relatives, and beaux, not to mention your enemies, makes you feel surprisingly benign towards all of them.

All of this being true, we come back to the need of a plan and the technique to carry it out – which we hope to give in the following pages.

CASES

Case I: Miss S. – While Miss S. is now plain, fifty, and entirely dependent on her salary as a teacher in a New York public school, thirty years ago she was the petted daughter of the leading banker in a small Maine city. When Papa died, leaving scandal in place of cash, there was head-shaking all up and down Penobscot Bay, but Miss S. merely screwed the knot of hair at the back of her head a little tighter, put on her sailor hat, and went to New York where she got herself a job before the neighbors had finished saying, 'Poor dear Susan.'

She still has the job, but she does not think of herself as an old-maid schoolteacher. Neither would you, if you met her. She has been a pioneer in everything pertaining to the equality of the sexes, from bloomers to picketing for Suffrage, and she's had a marvelous time. She continues to have it, since today, as usual, practically everything could do with a little reforming by people like Miss S.

Years ago, she found herself an apartment with three large, high-ceilinged rooms connected by a railroad hall, in an unfashionable and inconvenient section where rents are cheap. There she settled herself and her good old mahogany furniture, and there she still lives, not bewailing her loneliness, but congratulating herself on her independence.

As a matter of fact, she isn't lonely. Having spunk, humor, and intelligence, she also has innumerable women friends who smoke and discuss world problems around her fire in the winter and accompany her on the trips she takes in her second-hand Ford in the summer. They do not come on Sunday or Thursday nights, when Miss S. has a standing engagement with a near-sighted professor who has a wife in a sanitarium, whose books on mathematics are well-known in scholastic circles (and nowhere else), and who believes that Miss S. is beautiful.

In spite of living by one of the most underpaid professions in the world, Miss S. has been to Europe three times and to Mexico once, and three years ago she paid for the care of a tubercular pupil. She feels very sorry for her friends in Maine whose lives are limited to husbands and a trip to Portland.

Case II: Miss H. – Miss H., of Wilmington, is as rich as a bootlegger and as smart as paint and that is all we have to say for her. Her father got her the money and her mother turned her over to the best dressmaking houses, but nobody ever worked on her courage or character.

As an orphan, Miss H., languid and elegant, lives in stuffy and stately splendor, waiting for Something to Turn Up. What she expects is a husband, but all that actually does turn up is at best a party given by the dull type of person who sponges.

We wish that Miss S., or Mrs. C., could have a little of her money. Miss S. would go after a Cause, and Mrs. C. would make Cook County sit up and blink, and either course would be superior to Miss H.'s apathetic waiting.

Case III: Mrs. C. – Mrs. C. was brought up in a

small town in Illinois, and lived in Chicago through her ten years of married life, absorbing sophistication like a sponge. When her husband died, she weighed the advantages of being a widow in one place or the other and decided that her choice was between frills in her home town and necessities in Chicago. Knowing herself better than most of us do, she took the frills and returned, sleek and slim in widow's weeds, to her native home.

There are those who think that Mrs. C. does not always distinguish between living with an air and putting on airs. (We wish they would clear up the difference for us.) Whichever Mrs. C. does, she does with gusto. Her white house, as nearly like one she once saw in the movies as possible, has lemon-yellow blinds outside and a Chinese-red floor inside. (The painter has been heard to say that Mrs. C. is just a little crazy.) She never serves ice-cream at her parties, and she has the only hostess gown nearer than Rockford.

Most of the town is intrigued rather than irritated, believing that Mrs. C. is not putting them in their place, but merely living as she enjoys living. When guests come, they are taken to see the view from the hill outside the town, Borden's milk factory, and

Mrs. C. Her cotton chintz evening dresses, silver snoods, Victorian curls, white rugs, footless bed, and odd menus furnish more conversation than the daily papers. She has become a Character and will some day become a Legend. And since Mrs. C. loves popularity and adores fame, and would have had little of either in Chicago, we salute her as a lady who knew what she wanted and got it.

CHAPTER TWO

WHO DO
YOU THINK YOU ARE?

YOU have probably noticed that the lady of your acquaintance who thinks of herself as a duchess may cause a good many laughs, but usually, in the main, is treated like a duchess – in so far, at least, as her friends know how a duchess should be treated. It is equally true that it is the lady who expects orchids who gets them, while you and I are pinning on a single gardenia.

With this in mind, you can figure out for yourself just what you'll become with a mental picture of

'Poor little me, all alone in a big bad world.' Not only will you soon actually be all alone; you will also be an outstanding example of the super-bore.

If you are in the habit of thinking of yourself as a widow or a spinster, this, too, is something to get over as speedily as possible. Both words are rapidly becoming extinct – or, at least, being relegated to another period, like bustle and reticule. A woman is now a woman, just as a man is a man, and expected to stand on her own feet, as he (supposedly) stands on his.

There is not much use, however, in thinking of yourself as Ina Claire and then acting like Zenobia Frome, or any other mournful character in fiction. It's a good idea, first of all, to get over the notion (if you have it) that your particular situation is a little bit worse than anyone else's. This point of view has been experienced by every individual the world over at one time or another, except perhaps those who will experience it next year.

Another good rule for any liver-alone is not to feel hurt when Mary Jones doesn't ask you to her dinner-party, or when Cousin Joe fails to drop in to see you. It probably wasn't convenient for either of them. Perhaps Mary Jones *does* owe you more invitations than she owed her other guests. And undoubtedly Cousin Joe ought to care about how you are getting along. But nobody meant to hurt your feelings. Everybody, these days, is busy – or thinks she (or he) is. And the truth is that the very act of establishing yourself as a woman alone made you something of an obligation – which, we may as well face, is likely to lessen your desirability a shade.

This will be a surprise if you are among those who moved into a single apartment with a romantic picture of yourself as a game little woman on her own – and expected everyone else to see you in the same light. As a matter of fact, your friends (to say nothing of your family) would find it a lot simpler if you'd acquired a husband instead of a desire to Live Your Own Life.

Their attitude is your next hurdle. And the rule for getting over it is: Never, never, *never* let yourself feel that anybody ought to do anything for you. Once you become a duty you also become a nuisance. Be surprised and pleased, if you like, at gifts, invitations, and other attentions. Or, better still, take them casually. But don't let anyone suspect if you miss them. Your friends firmly intend to come across with attentions – and generally do, but not until you have cried yourself to sleep three or four times, decided that your sister-in-law has undermined your brother's affections, and made up your mind that you will never feel quite the same towards your best friend.

These unpleasantnesses are considerably lessened if you expect them. It helps surprisingly to know that the most popular people have had similar experiences and that the Queen of Sheba would occasionally feel snubbed if she were in your position. It may even prevent your getting a complex about being neglected – a fatal point of view, and entirely avoidable.

The solution is, of course, to get there first. Ask Cousin Joe to drop in for tea before you're quite sure in your own mind that he's neglecting you. Ask the young man you met at dinner, who said he'd like to call, to stop by for a cocktail before you know whether he's forgotten you or not. Or better still, fill your time up with such amusing things that you will forget all about both Cousin Joe and the lagging caller. Remember that nothing is so damaging to self-esteem as waiting for a telephone or door-bell that doesn't ring.

As a matter of fact, you will probably have to

muffle both door-bell and telephone if you can put yourself over as a gay, interesting, and up-to-date person. Anyone can, if she has sufficient determination. You can't sit at home and wait for these qualities to descend upon you like a light from Heaven, but you can acquire them by means of a little serious concentration on friends, hobbies, parties, books, and almost anything else that keeps you interested. Any one of them – or, more accurately, any ten or twelve – will also keep you interesting. But you've got to have variety. Your specialties, or hobbies, are all very well (we're going to say a lot about them later on), but they're not enough. Every woman should have a smattering of knowledge about practically everything. The half-dozen things you may have time to know thoroughly (if you're very ambitious) will amuse and broaden you and make you a better talker, but they will not make you a better companion, which involves being a good listener. To listen well, you must have at least a vague idea of what the other fellow is talking about (unless you're really clever). It is both boring and irritating for him to have to adapt his conversation so that you can understand it.

The same need of at least a dusting of knowledge

applies when you go to plays, concerts, operas, radio, lectures, sermons, art exhibits, foreign places, and almost everything else that we can think of except motion-pictures, which are usually fool-proof (and need to be). But more than that, it does wonders to your morale. No one can be in the know about most of the current goings-on without feeling that she is, after all, a pretty smart person – a feeling that even the best of us soon communicate to our friends. (What the friends think will be taken up in the next chapter.)

One last point about this mental picture of yourself: you won't get far unless you resemble it at least slightly. It takes a genius to make an impression in run-down heels and an unbecoming hat. You need good clothes and grooming – unless, of course, you think of yourself as a poor thing; in which case, it's nothing to us whether you get far or not. Our vote is for a little pampering – as much, in fact, as can be squeezed out of your schedule and your budget, and we have often noticed that it is *not* the ladies with the uncrowded schedules and large budgets who look the best.

We are not going into the subject of clothes. There is no reason why the woman who lives alone should look any different from the woman who doesn't, and every reason why she shouldn't. But do have some really smart street costumes – surprisingly, they can cost as little as dowdy ones, and practically no one's morale can overcome an outfit that's all wrong. Do have some evening clothes with *swish*, and – very specially – do have at least one nice seductive tea-gown to wear when you're alone (or when you're not, if you feel like it).

Do go in for cosmetics in a serious way. Not any old cream, but the right creams. The right coiffure, too, and the right nail-polish, and all the other beauty tricks that make you feel elegant. This is the kind of pampering that pays.

There are other good kinds: a glass of sherry and an extra special dinner charmingly served on a night when you're tired and all alone; bath salts in your tub and toilet-water afterward; a new and spicy book when you're spending an evening in bed; a trim little cotton frock that flatters you on an odd morning when you decide to be violently domestic. The notion that it 'doesn't matter because nobody sees you,' with the dull meals and dispirited clothes that follow in its wake, has done more damage than all the floods of springtime.

CASES

Case IV: Mrs. R. — Twenty years ago, Mrs. R. was a young and rather gawky young girl who lived in a small Southern town and read fashion publications surreptitiously. After her family had retired for a night of well-earned slumber, she could be seen holding a page from a magazine in one hand, while the other held the divan couch cover draped around her in the lines depicted in the photograph on the page. In time, she decided not merely to be smart, but exactly into what type of smart woman she would turn herself.

Today, she might be taken for the original of a fashion drawing in one of the magazines she once smuggled into the old family homestead (which, we are sorry to say, she seldom visits). She is thirty-five and has a score of three divorces. She has, also, an Elizabeth Arden figure, her rather ugly features are groomed to the last hair's-breadth, her hair is curled in a style a week ahead of the latest coiffure, and her finger-nails are a shade of scarlet that you and I may get around to next season.

But do not think that Mrs. R. acquired her chic painlessly. She hasn't had a square meal since

Coolidge was president, and there was a time when she never had but two outfits in her closet at once, in order to have both perfect. She has never wavered in her belief that fashion was more than food or quantity in clothes, however; and her job as a stylist is meat and drink to her in any case.

She lives her job literally, carrying it into every detail of her daily life, from the smart lawyer who got her Reno divorce to the Laurencin picture over the mirrored mantel in her very modern Sutton Place apartment. She goes in for Schiaparelli clothes, Frankl furniture, white pottery, and elegant though slightly effeminate young men.

Her enemies call her hard-boiled, and you might not like her friends or her way of living any better than we do, but we know of no one who has brought to life the Portrait of Herself as she wanted to be more successfully than Mrs. R. The moral of the story, if any, is that it's a good idea to pick a more attractive model of what you want to be before you start.

Case V: Miss J. – This is a sad story of a young woman who sees herself as a martyr and has never noticed that however appealing the role may be to the player, it is a terrible bore to everyone else.

Miss J. always gets the small end of everything, and the worst seat on the bus. Just try to give her anything else! She lives all, all alone, which is somehow dreadfully pathetic in Miss J.'s case, though rather pleasant in others. She has a passion for the past and lives in the family mausoleum, surrounded by an aura of virtue and relics of the days when her mother was alive. She seems to be in chronic mourning for all the relatives who have died within her memory and in a state of chronic resentment over the neglect of all those who haven't died. We don't blame the relatives, and we would enjoy giving Miss J. and her house a thorough airing.

Case VI: Miss A. – Miss A. was brought up by pious parents in Brooklyn, and up to the age of thirty she thought that smart clothes were something for somebody else – and looked it. Not being encouraged to give time, thought, or money to anything so frivolous as fashion, she never recognized a new style till she had seen it for so many weeks that it was beginning to be an old style; and her casually bought wardrobes usually turned out to have a brown coat, a black hat, and a blue dress.

At thirty, however, Miss A. got a position in Cleveland, her immediate superior being a lady who knew her fashions. It soon became evident that Miss A. had better do likewise if she wished to continue in favor. She therefore put her really excellent mind to the study of how to be chic on a small salary, with surprising results.

This was five years ago, and, while Miss A. is still no Mrs. Harrison Williams, you would look twice at her as an unusually well-dressed woman in any restaurant. Her clothes are what smart women are just buying and not what they were wearing month before last. Not only do her hat, coat, and dress

match – or contrast in a way that gives a fillip to her costume – but this applies also to her gloves, shoes, and bag. More amazing still, Miss A.'s annual outlay for clothes is no more than it was in Brooklyn. Having really informed herself on what is what and how to plan and buy a wardrobe, Miss A. has now built up a more or less permanent foundation – tailored suits that are good for several seasons; a top-coat and an evening wrap that she can wear for a number of years; country clothes, sweaters, sports shoes, and similar things that do not date. She has, also, an underlying color scheme, so that her accessories are interchangeable.

Miss A.'s opinion of herself has improved as much as her appearance.

CHAPTER THREE

WHEN A
LADY NEEDS A FRIEND

As we have already suggested, one of the great
secrets of living alone successfully is not to live alone
too constantly. A reasonably large circle of friends
and enemies whom you can see when you want to,
and will often see when you don't want to, is an
important asset. Anybody can acquire it, but it
takes a little doing.

Perhaps you have them already – but just wait till
you're established in your one-woman apartment,
and see how rapidly they fade out of the picture

unless you do what is known as Keeping Up Your End.

This keeping-up requires far more planning in a small establishment than in a large one. In most big families, somebody is always asking somebody else to a meal, and parties are a matter of spontaneous combustion. Also, you are apt to be included in invitations to other members of your family – all of which makes a gay life comparatively effortless.

But, in your own solitary ménage, parties won't happen unless you plan them, and there won't be many guests unless you invite them. Moreover, you won't be a guest yourself unless you are also a hostess. Why should you be?

The most popular woman in the world might be invited to Mrs. Smith's house two – or even three – times without a return engagement. But it's a safe bet that, unless she does something for Mrs. Smith, she won't be invited a fourth time. If she were, she wouldn't go. The old-fashioned notion that single women are objects of social charity was killed in the War.

Nor is the invitation to Mrs. Smith enough. You've got to give her – to say nothing of Mr. Smith – a good time when she gets there.

This is really a simple matter. The best parties (we are not referring to Beaux Arts Balls or liquor marathons, but to parties of four to perhaps eight) are not trick affairs. They consist chiefly of guests and food that mix well and drinks that are well mixed.

Don't think that your establishment is too simple even for this. You can get over any embarrassment you may feel in this respect by entertaining, first, guests who are in the same fix as you – or worse. Preferably worse. Perhaps you do *not* live in an eight-room apartment with a large and handsome dining-room and two maids. A four-room apartment with a foyer that does double-duty as a dining-room, and one maid, may be just as chic as the larger one – if you know how to make it so. Or perhaps, instead of the four-room apartment, yours is a two-room affair. Many a clever woman is a charming hostess at a refectory table set in the window of her living-room, with a maid who comes in for company occasions. Or perhaps you live in a one-room apartment, and your kitchen is a hole in the wall. You can still feel like a grande dame if you entertain a lady living in a single bedroom with no kitchen whatsoever. In fact, with ingenuity and the things that now come out of cans, you can give her a Park Avenue dinner.

The point is to get her, and her sisters (not to mention her brothers), to come and to like it. Singly, if that's easier, but often. She'll have to ask you back. And so, with a little persistency, begins a series of activities that may lead to anything, but will certainly put an end to loneliness.

Of course, it is not parties, but companionship that is essential to happiness. Every woman needs to have friends who drop in for tea or cocktails or supper, and who ask her to drop in. She needs friends with whom to share expeditions, friends to whom she can pour out her enthusiasms and troubles and show off her new hats and her old beaux.

If you live where you've always lived, you already have a circle of friends – or ought to have. Then, it's largely a matter of rearranging them. In the first place, if your solitary state is recent, don't expect to see as much of the married ones as you used to. And don't be so hurt by the new state of affairs that you spoil the party when they do include you. Remember, you're a lot of trouble to them anyway. And you probably wouldn't have enjoyed being a fifth wheel – or a seventh, or any other number that is disturbing to bridge games, dinner-tables, tête-à-têtes, or dancing. Above all, don't get to be one of those tiresome women who drop in on their relatives' parties and expect to cut into a game, while some invited guest sits by and watches.

It's a good idea to collect Odd Numbers like yourself, the way Mr. Frick collected paintings. You can build up quite a coterie if you take enough trouble, mix your friends intelligently, and show a little shrewdness as to when to invite them, and what for. Include as few relatives as possible in one group, on the principle that it's infinitely better for a Lone Female to offend her relatives by not inviting them enough, than to bore her relations by inviting them too often. In other words, it's better to be a snob than a hanger-on.

If you have come recently to a new town, your difficulties are greater, but by no means hopeless. And this is true whether your contacts are through the Junior League, or the sales-girls in a department store. If you haven't any contacts, put your hat right on and go out and start making them. You probably have, at least, a fourth cousin to look up or a few letters to present. If not, there are always business women's organizations, dancing classes, literary courses, political clubs, churches, Y.W.C.A.s, poetry groups, bridge lessons, musical circles, skating clubs, riding-classes, college-extension courses, and what-not. Be a Communist, a stamp collector, or a Ladies' Aid worker if you must, but for heaven's sake, be something.

When you are something, do something about it. Pick out your logical prey, and pounce. This process is called 'going half-way' and often means going two-thirds of the way or more. (It does not, however, mean going too far.)

A good beginning is to find out what the other person likes to do. You then intimate that you like to do it, too, and after some parleying eventually reach, 'Let's do it together.'

Games are among the best get-together aids yet invented. Tennis, golf, bridge, backgammon. You might even polish up your croquet and take on Mr. Woollcott. It makes very little difference what you play, but it's a good idea to play it really well. If you find yourself marooned in Woodbine, Iowa, and the favorite game there is Parchesi, don't be above giving a little serious attention to Parchesi. There may be only a comparatively few smart games, but there are innumerable good games, and an ability to play them is insurance against boredom.

Food is, of course, the Great Uniter. While only a very rare party can survive dull refreshments, people are almost always friendly if you feed them well enough – well enough meaning, not quantity, but quality, as applied to the standards of the guests. There is probably no field with a greater range between provincialism and sophistication than that of the dinner-table. You can be as funny serving caviar in the sticks as serving candlestick salad on Park Avenue. But over a really delicious, well-planned meal (which we will discuss in a later chapter), friendships can blossom like the dandelion, while a reputation for a good cuisine is an almost certain step towards popularity.

A course in cooking may do more than a course in conversation, since the perfect hostess is, after all, not so much the one who is good at talking as the one who is good at making her guests talk. Nor does good cooking mean elaborate cooking, even in the most sophisticated circles – what with Lady Mendl serving corned-beef hash to Nobility, and scrambled eggs and sausages being favorite dishes at the smartest débutante parties. As with so many things, it's a matter of being in the know.

We have left the real crux of the problem till the last, feeling that it's a delicate matter. For the truth is that if you're interesting, you'll have plenty of friends;

and if you're not, you won't — unless you're very, very rich. Fortunately, the first is easily accomplished, and we hope to tell you how in a later chapter.

CASES

Case VII: Miss MacD. — Both Miss MacD. and her salary as a stenographer are diminutive, and Miss MacD., in addition, is a timid young person of twenty-two or -three. For several years, she lived in an inexpensive boarding-house in Detroit, slipping in and out unobtrusively and growing more and more convinced that life was a very lonely business. Then through a series of coincidences she discovered that several girls in the firm where she worked earned even less than she did and got around no more.

This cheered Miss MacD. immensely, just as it would cheer you. No sooner did she begin to feel sorry for the others than she became a new woman. In a short time, she found herself a one-room apartment with a nice view of somebody's back yard, had some furniture sent from home, and equipped her kitchenette elegantly from the ten-cent store. She then found that she had a flair for making such things as curried eggs and green salad, and she began to invite everyone who couldn't possibly give her an inferiority complex to come to supper.

Miss MacD.'s apartment is now the gathering-place of the clan, and she wonders how she ever happened to think that Detroit was lonely. She goes to movies, to a bowling club in a church parish house, and to dances, and her free evenings are few enough to be pleasures.

Case VIII: Mrs. P. – Mrs. P. is an Englishwoman who found herself a stranger in an unfamiliar country and with very little money, at the age of thirty-eight. She had, however, an enormous fund of common sense and cheerfulness, and with these assets she proceeded to make herself a new life.

After getting a job, her second procedure was to follow every available road towards making friends, and her next was to make a background to which they would be attracted. This has necessarily gone through various phases, but Mrs. P. has now acquired a home that she hopes will be permanent. Expense being a very definite item, it is some distance from town, and she has a long daily trip – but Mrs. P. has learned that you have to pay for everything in this world and has decided that her present arrangement is worth the price.

The house, which began as a ready-made affair and has had two additions, is a simple clapboard building on a point of land that extends into Long Island Sound. There are a porch, a garden, and a pier, and, with this equipment and very little additional expense, Mrs. P. has a set-up to which practically everybody she meets is delighted to come – for a swim, a sun-bath, and tea, if nothing more. This advantageous arrangement, added to Mrs. P.'s own charm and the attractive way in which she lives, has enabled her to pick and choose, until now she has a wide and interesting circle of friends who make her winters as delightful as she makes their summers and week-ends.

Case IX: Miss L. – Miss L. is the daughter of a celebrity, and the first eighteen years of her life she was in great demand because of her close connection with Fame. Her father, unhappily, has now been dead for several years, but Miss L. has not yet learned the fickleness of popularity and is still under the impression that people are dying to meet her. She accepts invitations with regal condescension and, once at a party, waits expectantly for an onslaught of attention that doesn't come. Miss L. always convinces herself that people didn't get her name, and she wouldn't believe you if you told her that the younger generation have never heard of her father.

She doesn't feel that there is any need for her to return invitations. Doesn't she honor the parties by going to them and isn't that enough?

It is enough of you, Miss L. Pretty soon there won't be any invitations for you to honor.

Case X: Miss N. – Miss N. is a pink and plump lady with ideas as large as her front façade, who came to New York from Alabama bent on conquest and pursued success and the men she met with equal determination. Her stride, acquired in the open spaces, has carried her from poverty to comparative prosperity, but has not yet enabled her to overtake any of the gentlemen. Miss N.'s salary is now large enough so that she could have an entertaining life if she could get her mind off her unfulfilled ambition. For some time, she has admitted being forty, but she is still pink, plump, and pretty. People like her until the gleam of the huntress comes into her eye and sends her men friends off in alarm. She gives excellent parties – although she seldom enjoys them herself, since they fail to produce results. She has a pleasant apartment and can serve a better dinner and mix a better cocktail than you or I. She goes to plays and concerts and to other people's week-ends – in fact, she gets around more than a lot of good wives.

But more and more a horrid little thought is intruding itself into Miss N.'s mind and spoiling any party. Perhaps, it occurs to her, she will always be Miss N.

Well, what if you are, Miss N.? There may still be those in Alabama who look upon an unmarried state as an affliction, but in New York it is at most a very minor ailment.

CHAPTER FOUR

ETIQUETTE FOR
A LONE FEMALE

QUESTION: When a woman gives a dinner-party at her house or apartment, and takes her guests on to a play, is it correct for her to pay for taxis to and from the theater?

Answer: According to etiquette books, yes. Actually, no. The men guests always pay. You might go through the motions feebly, but they will know that you know they'll get there first, so it's not worth making much of an effort.

Question: How late is it proper for a woman

living alone to entertain a man friend, and how can she get him to go at the correct time?

Answer: The correct time depends on the lady and also on the time of arrival. Ten-forty-five P.M. might seem scandalous to your Aunt Hattie, and three-thirty A.M. be disconcertingly early to the girl on the floor below. In either case, the time the man arrived should be a factor. No call should turn into an endurance test, and four or five hours of being a perfect listener will make any hostess feel like a runner-up in a nine-days' bicycle race.

As far as propriety goes, a man might come for dinner and stay long enough to take the milk in, and no offense to anyone. (This, we admit, is improbable.) Or it might be time for him to go after the first highball.

How to get rid of him depends entirely on your type. However, before making the attack, it's a good idea to decide whether you want him to go for good or merely for the occasion. In the first instance, it's a simple matter. Just tell him so in good plain English. (This will sometimes work in the second instance; but you must be sure of your man.)

If you want him to come again soon, a little tact is usually wiser. You might begin with, 'Let me get you a glass of water (nothing stronger) – it's hours since you had that highball.' This will get you both up and give you the advantage. You can keep on standing, which will eventually wear down any man (if you don't drop first).

There is little danger that you will have to call the elevator man or open the window and scream. It may happen, but don't get your hopes up. You have to be pretty fascinating.

Question: When a lady entertains a married couple and an extra man at her house at dinner, how should she seat them? It would seem natural to put him opposite the hostess, but does not this suggest that he is the man of the house?

Answer: This is one of those unimportant details of etiquette that are far too much stressed. What does it matter where he sits? Seat him so that he – and you and the other guests – are comfortable and happy. Having seated him, take it for granted that he's in the right place, and no one will think about it one way or another. If you make excuses, your guests will wonder if you *were* right.

If you must have someone decide the matter for you – why not put the other lady opposite you and the man you know least well on your right?

ETIQUETTE FOR A LONE FEMALE

Question: What is expected in the way of tips from a woman traveling alone to Europe or on a cruise? Will it not be understood if she tips less than a man would, or the members of a party or family?

Answer: Why should it? A woman traveling alone is just as much trouble as anyone else. Usually, she's a lot more trouble, as she expects more service. However, any good traveler expects a great deal of service, knowing that nothing adds more to the comfort of any trip. But she, as well as he, pays for it.

For the usual service on a crossing to Europe, or a cruise of about the same length, each person gives five dollars to the room steward, stewardess, and dining steward, and three dollars to the deck steward. Any other tips are given for special service at the time it is rendered. It's a good idea to tip the head dining steward, too, before the first meal and to have a little talk as to where and with whom you are to sit. If you're out for a gay trip (and why not?), let him get the idea along with the tip. This gesture will sometimes accomplish wonders.

Question: Do you suggest a Woman's Club as the best solution of the problem of a woman who wishes to entertain men friends occasionally?

Answer: We do not. That is, if it is a possible

thing for a woman to entertain at home. You may get as good food in some clubs as you would in the average house, but the effects are not to be compared. There's nothing like a good domestic background for producing results. The most hardened man will weaken before those little home touches and a becoming tea-gown. If you can't supply the background, however, or don't want the results, join the club by all means. It will save you a lot of trouble in any case.

Question: Is it permissible for a youngish un-chaperoned woman living alone to wear pajamas when a gentleman calls?

Answer: Assuming that she knows one pajama from another, it is entirely permissible. There are, however, sleeping pajamas, beach pajamas, lounging pajamas, and hostess pajamas. The first two are not designed to wear when receiving anybody, masculine or feminine. The last type is correct for wear when your most conservative beau calls, even though he belongs to the old school and winces when a lady smokes. The third variety comes in all sorts of shadings, from an almost-sleeping type to a practically hostess pajama. Those with a leaning towards the bed are suitable only for feminine guests, while the others would not shock Bishop Manning.

CHAPTER FIVE

YOUR LEISURE, IF ANY

EVERY woman who lives alone has a problem in her leisure hours, and this does not mean that she is no Greta Garbo. You might have two dinner invitations every night in the week and three proposals on Sunday, and you would still have this problem. For no woman can accept an invitation every night (to say nothing of the proposal every Sunday) and not come to grief. You've got to stay home part of the time, and staying home alone is as different from settling down with a book and a husband in the armchair opposite as a game of solitaire is from a game of poker.

Even if you are as strong as a horse and an exception to this rule, you probably spend plenty of breakfasts, luncheons, evenings, Sundays, and holidays entertaining yourself. Are you really entertained?

Anyone with any gumption can be. The first rule is to have several passionate interests. There must be at least a million to choose from – like collecting stamps, or reading up on the famous mistresses in French history, or writing good or bad plays, or doing needlepoint, or learning fancy skating. You should have at least one that keeps you busy at home and another that takes you out. Just dabbling in them isn't enough, either. They will not be really efficacious until you're the kind of enthusiast who will stay home to follow the first type in spite of a grand invitation, or go out and follow the second in spite of wind, sleet, or rain.

Don't worry if you find yourself being a bit of a bore on some of your hobbies. Everybody is occasionally a bore to at least some of his friends. The most brilliant scientists are not entertaining to most ladies, nor do the most brilliant ladies always amuse the scientists. And hasn't your mind wandered when even your most fascinating beau talked about stocks and bonds and you wanted him to talk about you? But when you get to the stage of 'holding forth,' you will at least fascinate yourself, and you will also be on the road to becoming an authority. This may prove profitable, even though your hobby is trained fleas or the Yogi cult. In general, however, it's wiser not to be too quaint in your choice of enthusiasms. Something like collecting antiques or growing gardenias will draw more kindred spirits, and also more congenial ones.

Antiquing is particularly satisfactory, as it serves both at home and abroad and stirs your sense of adventure even in these days of great exploitations. A good way to begin is to spend several lunch hours a week, if you're a working girl – several afternoons, if you aren't – visiting antique stores and antique departments. You can make quite an art of sounding interested and drawing out the saleslady without spending a nickel – which is not so objectionable as it sounds, since every now and then Fate will turn on you and put in your path a bit of glass or mahogany that you can't get along without.

The knowledge you acquire must be bolstered up by homework, which gets to be fun, and eventually you will know enough to get the thrill of a lifetime out of dropping into second-hand stores and junk shops on queer back streets and poking among dusty bits of cut glass and broken furniture till you come on a bit of real Sandwich glass or an old Duncan Phyfe sewing-table. Usually, this will turn out next day to be a reproduction, but you will have the thrill anyway – and every now and then you will actually be right. All of this leads inevitably to a passion for auctions, and for motoring around the country and stopping at every shop with a sign reading 'Antiques,' and it makes travel several times more adventurous – not to mention the charm it adds to your house and the conversation it supplies at your dinners.

The hobbies your friends will appreciate most are astrology, numerology, palmistry, reading hand-writing, and fortune-telling by cards (or anything else). In practicing any of these, you have to give your exclusive attention to the other person, which invariably fascinates him. Any one of these accomplish-ments will, therefore, make you an asset at a party and enable you to hold any man's interest for at least half an hour. By discovering unusual characteristics in his palm or in the stars that govern him, you can do much better than that. This hobby will probably entertain your friends more than it will you, however.

You might go in for collecting little china dogs, old bottles, snuff-boxes, or even monkeys. Collecting almost anything is a compensating hobby. Or you might take up Greek or tap-dancing, genealogy or making jewelry. The idea, as you may gather, is to have some hobbies.

Even a number of hobbies will not – or should not – fill all your leisure, however, and, when you are planning the rest, it's a good idea to divide your time intelligently into hours spent alone and hours spent in entertainment. Both should be taken in moderation, and balanced rations are best. This is not always easy, as invitations have a way of coming in bunches. Fortunately, you can usually get a rain-check on some of them. Loneliness is as apt to be the result of exhaustion as of solitude – but too much solitude is just as bad, even though you spend it excitingly. Get into the habit of planning your week ahead, instead of drifting along, thinking something pleasant will turn up. Often, it doesn't, and it's too late then to get hold of really amusing people – who probably *have* made their plans in advance. Besides, nice engagements are fun to look forward to, and a full schedule makes you feel, yourself, that you are more of a person.

This full schedule involves a certain number of friends. We admit that we are getting a little tiresome on this subject, but we stick to our story that friends are important. Hermits and other self-sufficient people may be geniuses (we doubt it) and contribute greatly to the scientific knowledge of the world, but they contribute practically nothing to its entertainment and have a very dull time themselves. Most people's minds are like ponds and need a constantly fresh stream of ideas in order not to get stagnant. The simplest way to accomplish this is to exchange your ideas, if any, with your friends and acquaintances, cribbing as many as possible from books, plays, and newspaper columns and passing them off as your own. Anyone who does this well is considered a brilliant conversationalist. If you do it extra well, you are a Wit.

Even if your aim is merely to reach an average as an amusing person, you'll need to keep at it. However, the requisites aren't difficult – a few discriminating moments spent on the morning paper, a few varied and well-chosen magazines read thoroughly, at least one good book a week, and a reasonable amount of 'getting around' should do the trick. But you must keep an open mind about what you read and where you go. Favorite authors and one favorite movie house are all very well in moderation, but they can become old-lady habits if you don't watch out. It's much better to read a few books that you don't like, but that some good critic does, and see a few plays that you detest, but that everyone is talking about. Following one of the good literary and dramatic critics is a good habit, in any case – it keeps you up-to-date on current goings-on and prevents you from wasting time on books and plays that aren't worth the trouble.

If you're one of those people who smile in a superior way about self-improvement courses, you might do a little self-investigating for a change. So many people with this attitude could do very well with considerable improving. We admit that few courses will turn you into somebody else overnight, or even change you from Bridesmaid to Bride, or enable you to impress the head waiter with your *savoir faire* in a couple of months. But we can think of a lot of poorer ways of spending your leisure than dipping into the good ones.

There is one course in New York, for instance, in Personal Adequacy – and if there is anyone who couldn't take that with benefit, we've never met her or him either. The person who runs it, surprisingly, does *not* think that she can teach everyone everything, from ethics to posture to charm. Her method is merely to let you talk to her about yourself, while she makes mental note of the things that seem wrong with you. A few days later, you are told to go to see somebody else – a voice specialist or a fashion consultant or what-have-you, and you deliver another personal monologue, no doubt enjoying yourself thoroughly. After a few such sessions have been reported in full to the first interviewer and mulled over carefully, you are given a chart that tells you all the things that are wrong and also all the things that are right, and how to overcome the first and emphasize the second. You know that already? Or do you? And what, if anything, do you do about it? Just think it over for a while before you decide too finally that your personal liabilities are crosses that have to be borne.

Perhaps, after that, you'll have found another way of spending your leisure.

A reasonable amount of travel ought, of course, to be listed among the necessities. (An unreasonable amount if you can manage it.) If you don't agree with this, there is something wrong with you, and you should see a doctor or a minister or at least read a few travel books and folders. All normal people should get wrought up now and then over the fact that there are wild orchids in Brazil that they may never see, and temple bells in Mandalay that they may never hear, and beautiful Balinese maidens and incredible Tibetan Lamaseries that they are likely to miss altogether. These being out of the question, there is still Atlantic City, if you live in the East and call that travel, and Ensenada, or Palm Springs, if you live in the West, and points of interest all the way between, not to mention Canada and Mexico and cruises for any type and pocketbook.

Perhaps all this seems a bit extravagant – a program for a woman who has arrived, and not for one who is on the way or who has just started. It is true that you have to make your life fit your income. But you can apply all of our pet principles on a very small salary. You can have a good meal for the price of a bad one, and furnish a living-room charmingly for as little as bad taste would cost. (Bad taste can be very, very expensive.) With a reasonable amount of ingenuity, you can have a marvelous time on practically nothing.

The larger cities offer the most variety in this respect – New York, probably, more than any other in this country. But the smaller ones cost less, and each has its own advantages.

There is no limit to the things you can do inexpensively in New York, if you're sufficiently up and doing. Have you, for instance, ever been to the movie house way up-town where twenty-year-old pictures are shown, knee-high skirts and all, and elegant prizes are handed out, especially on Saturday nights? Have you ever been to a Yiddish theater, with its really fine acting, on the lower East Side? Or to a Spiritualist meeting on the upper West Side? Have you ever been to the Flea Circus, or played games with a nickel for stakes on Broadway? (Have an escort for the last one.)

Have you hunted up the little French boarding-house-like restaurants where gourmets gather and dinner costs next to nothing; or the Italian restaurants, or Spanish ones, or Russian, Turkish, or Armenian ones where food is both cheap and good?

Have you heard the finest New York organists play on Sunday afternoons, or the Russian Orthodox Cathedral choir sing, or been to the poetry symposiums at Saint-Marks-in-the-Bouwerie?

Have you tried the swimming pools at the Y.W.C.A., or skated in Central Park, or joined a Public-Speaking Class? Have you ridden back and forth on a Staten Island ferry late on a winter afternoon, when lower New York sparkles across the harbor from every high window, like a theater back-drop?

Have you spent a spring Sunday out at Bronx Park, when millions of tulips or iris are in bloom and more kinds of lilac bushes than you knew existed? Or been to the Bronx Zoo, where even a grown-up should go once or twice? Or lunched beside the seals on a summer day when parasols dot the terrace of the Central Park cafeteria?

Have you walked across Brooklyn Bridge on a cool summer night, or across George Washington Bridge in the autumn when the Palisades are brilliant red and yellow? Have you been to Chinatown, or to a concert in the Park or in the Stadium?

Have you visited the great markets in the very early morning and seen the carts of green and yellow vegetables, and gold and scarlet fruits, and the stalls of various foods and drinks of every nation?

Do you use the Public Library nearest you – and really know how much it will do for you if you ask it to? Have you heard the six greatest preachers in the city? And been to lectures by some current celebrity?

Have you visited the American Wing at the Metropolitan and the Museum of the City of New York? Have you sat in the top balcony at the Opera, and haunted the cut-rate theater counters till you got cheap seats for at least two or three of the best shows in town? (Monday nights, for instance, you'll find them.)

Have you been to one prize-fight, and one radio broadcast, and maybe one burlesque? And what about the free art exhibits?

These are only a few of the things you could do on a factory-hand's salary. If you've lived in New York a year, and done even most of them, you haven't been bored. If you've lived in New York and done none at all – then, if you are bored, blame it on your own lack of initiative and not on circumstances.

CASES

Case XI: Miss T. – Miss T. came to New York some years ago from a small town in New Hampshire, bringing an assortment of small-town traits along with her – but you wouldn't believe it if you saw her today. For the last six years she has done her duty by her family by going home at Christmas, keeping her three-weeks' vacation intact for travel. For forty-nine weeks of the year she works hard, and on Sunday mornings she finds the most fascinating reading in the newspapers in the travel section. She has figured out every place that can be covered in twenty-one days and when and how you can do it most cheaply. Up to date, she has made boat trips to Caracas, Labrador, New Orleans, and Majorca, and visited Quebec and Florida by train.

On every trip, her one extravagance is a purchase for her apartment (several purchases, if possible), which, she says, will remind her of the trip when she's old and can't get around. Meanwhile they are both decorative and useful.

She has made at least one friend on every trip, and kept them all, which has meant innumerable luncheon- and dinner-dates when the friends arrive in New York, and several week-end invitations. And she herself has gained amazingly in poise, charm, and self-confidence.

Case XII: Miss G. – Miss G. has lived alone in Los Angeles for twelve years, eight of which were lonely and miserable. During these eight years, she lived in a boarding-house and worked as a section manager in a department store. Then an elderly relative from the East spent two weeks in town and took Miss G. to lunch and to dinner a half-dozen times. He was one of these gentlemen with a hobby that amounted to a passion – and it chanced, in this instance, to be photography. Finding Miss G. unusually responsive, he made her a parting gift of a very fine camera and urged her to go to a commercial school of photography in the evenings. This Miss G. did – and life became quite different. Within six months, she had won an amateur photographer's prize offered by a newspaper. Six months later she moved into a tiny apartment in order to have a small room (the kitchen – Miss G. is not domestic) for doing her own developing and printing. Not long after this, she got a commission (through the school) to try some fashion photography.

Miss G. now has her own studio and is a

professional photographer instead of a section manager. She has doubled her acquaintance and tripled her salary, but – far more important than this – her work makes it necessary for her to keep up on modern art, theaters, clothes, and anything else that comes into her field. She is now far more interested, and far more interesting, than ever before.

Case XIII: Miss B. – Two years ago, Miss B.'s position made it necessary for her to move from Buffalo to Chicago, where she had no friends whatever. She soon found a pleasant one-room-and-bath-dressing-room apartment, but the matter of getting to know people proved more of a problem. Miss B., however, though neither beautiful nor dashing and having a very limited salary, is a friendly young lady with resources.

After a few rather drab weeks, she took herself firmly in hand. She joined a Tuesday-night gymnasium class at the Y.W.C.A. and a Thursday-night class in Interior Decoration, and she budgeted her expenses so that she could go to a play or a good movie on Saturday nights. To back up her study of decoration, she spent at least half of her lunch hours visiting exhibitions, fine furniture shops, rooms arranged in the larger department stores, textile exhibits, and the Art

Institute. In addition, she mapped out a course in reading the books she'd always meant to read – and pursued it on free evenings.

Miss B. is beginning her third year in Chicago, but she knows more people than many natives and has so few free evenings that when she wants to read she makes a date with herself and goes to bed with her book. The nucleus of her circle of friends were met in her work and the two classes, and the rest are friends of the nucleus, or friends of the friends. She still, however, goes to class once a week. This year, it's tap-dancing.

Case XIV: Mrs. de W. – Mrs. de W. started a sensationally successful career when she was in her early twenties and kept right on for forty years, getting better and better. She worked like a farmhand during the whole period, and, when she retired at sixty-two, she looked it. Her friends, however, were more concerned about the sudden change in her activities then the gradual change in her appearance.

'How will you spend your time?' they asked with one accord.

'On the old chassis,' said Mrs. de W. 'On the poor old battered body.'

And so she does.

She has her breakfast in bed, late, leisurely, and comfortably. She lets nothing crowd out her regular weekly appointments for a shampoo, a scalp treatment, a wave, a facial, and a manicure. Two mornings a week, she spends in a health salon, where she exercises, sits in a cabinet bath, or lies under a sun-lamp to her heart's content. And on nights when she is very tried she has a masseuse come in and give her a long, soothing massage.

Last winter, Mrs. de W. went to Palm Beach and toasted herself under the sun. This year she plans to go to Palm Springs for the same purpose.

Her skin looks younger and more blooming than it has in forty years, and she has lost most of her hips and her tummy. At a tea recently, she entertained the guests by standing on her head.

Mrs. de W. is having an elegant time.

CHAPTER SIX

SETTING FOR A SOLO ACT

ANY home, of course, from a one-room apartment to a feudal manor, should be as charming, comfortable, and chic as possible – but this is several times as true of the one-woman affair as of any other. If someone lives with you, your mind is taken off your surroundings to some extent, even if you don't like the other person. (Especially so, in fact, there being nothing more engrossing than a good case of the kind of rage a housemate can arouse, unless perhaps it is a case of chronic irritation.) But living by

60

yourself, you're conscious of everything from badly chosen curtains to a crooked lamp-shade.

It's a good idea, then, to give some extra-special attention to your surroundings. The place you live should reflect your personality – and it will, whether you want it to or not. There is nothing more telltale than a room that has been lived in. It can be tailored or *chi-chi*, gracious or cute, masculine or feminine, ignorant or cultured. It will give you away to everyone who comes in, and it will influence your moods and your morale.

In the feudal manor, charm might be the first thing to go after, but, in your particular ménage, let's begin with chic. An up-to-the-minute quality matters enormously. In the first place, it's something that's essential in most jobs – and what you show in your job, you usually show in your background. Then, too, we have no patience with a woman who surrounds herself sentimentally with left-overs and decaying splendor and settles down to decay along with them. It's better to give an old mahogany sideboard to the Salvation Army than to live among too many reminders of the dear departed.

It's possible to keep the good antiques, however, and set them off with very modern curtains and accessories — and nothing could be smarter. But do have that modern look. No one can live very long in a musty atmosphere without getting a bit musty herself.

There has never been a time when it was so easy to make a house attractive. What with budget rooms in most of the stores, bargains in all of them, auction-rooms and second-hand stores overflowing, and 'styling' being applied to everything from oilcloth to grand pianos, the opportunities are practically unlimited. You can even acquire Good Taste, with a little concentration on the magazines dealing with interior decoration and visits to the best furniture stores and the American Wing.

Next to chic comes comfort. Many people put it first, and the results are what make us put it second. A room can be comfortable and very, very dull, or comfortable and depressingly stuffy. But, after all, it should be comfortable, and comfortable according to your own pet needs and peculiarities. Have the kind of chairs that you like to sit in, placed where you like to sit. Have furniture that can be grouped to fit the kind of entertaining you do. If you like to curl up, have a soft sofa and a huge chair or chaise longue —

and curl up. Have good lamps for reading in the spots where you'll use them; and little tables where they are most convenient; and a telephone within reach of your bed; and, if you have a maid, be sure to have a bell beside your bed and get into the habit of using it. This is your house, and it's probably the one place in the world where you can have things exactly as you please.

Third, comes charm, which is an intangible quality, like IT, that you'll have to acquire for yourself. Few things are more worth the effort, whether you're talking about charm in personality or charm in house furnishings. Or more worth the money. It need not cost much money, however. Taste is much more a matter of knowledge than of expense. If you know about line, color, composition, and the history behind furniture and furnishings, you have probably acquired taste automatically.

A little extravagance, however, is wise when it comes to such basic things as beds and mattresses and pillows and the larger items. They will probably last as long as you do, and you will get very, very sick of poor ones.

Just as important as the things you put in a room are the things you leave out. Clutter is now as out-of-date as modesty, and for just as good reasons. Clutter is confusing and wearing. It's hard to take care of. It's ugly in itself, and it makes its owner seem to belong to another period. Yet the Great Temptation – well, anyway, one of them – to most people living alone is to have too much furniture and too many what-nots. We've been in lots of feminine establishments from which you might have taken half the furnishings and given them to the nearest Thrift Shop – and achieved as much as if you'd called in a decorator.

This is partly because of sentiment and partly because the individual has usually moved from larger to smaller quarters and can't bear to give things up. This is one of those impractical economies we all go in for. We think we are saving things for Better Days, which frequently don't come. When they do, the things are out-of-date, and we can afford to buy new ones anyway.

The spirit of elimination is what has taken the wear and tear out of housekeeping. This – and the Disappearance of the Attic. The good old-fashioned attic with its boxes and trunks and packages that had to be moved and sorted and gone over must have given many a woman more gray hairs than her eight children, including the triplets. (They didn't have quintuplets in the days of attics.) You probably have no attic. If you have, your single-blessedness gives you no excuse whatever for not keeping it practically empty. Better still, use it as a ping-pong room.

Apply the same principle to any room, closet, and cupboard, and you've gone a long way toward achieving charm, comfort, and chic. Remember that there is no law requiring a picture in every wall space (too many of even the best pictures make a room look busy); that, in the main, table-covers and bureau scarfs have gone the way of all fashions; and that knickknacks are only smart when they're few and well-chosen.

It would be foolish to try to tell you what you *should* have. This is *your* background and setting, and it must depend on your taste, purse, and circumstances. If you don't know, go out and find out. Go to exhibitions – of rooms, and paintings, and ceramics, and all the allied arts. Some of the best ones to be seen are free. Even if you live in a furnished room, it's a good idea to know Queen Anne from Early American and whether a bergère is something to wear or to sit on.

It's more important, still, of course, if you furnish your own apartment. For a skillful mixture of periods may be as charming and sophisticated as anything done by Syrie Maugham, while an ignorant mixture can be terrible.

Whatever you decide on, don't do it half-heartedly. Your setting, if you live alone, matters much more than if you had a husband or even a lover. And your standards of living should be about ten points higher than if you lived with somebody else. The woman who treats herself like an aristocrat seems aristocratic to other people, and the woman who is sloppy at home inevitably slips sometimes in public.

It's all very well to take some friends out to the kitchen and let them stir up a midnight supper; but never, never, have snack meals by yourself on the kitchen table. No one's morale can stand them long. (If you don't want to set a table, fix a tray, with your best linen and china, and take it to a comfortable chair beside the window.) Never let the curtains go in your bedroom, because 'no one sees them.' Don't economize on flowers, or a single flower for the living-room, even though only you will enjoy them.

SETTING FOR A SOLO ACT

One of the great advantages of your way of living is that you *can* be alone when you want to. Lots of people never discover what a pleasure this can be. Perhaps it was because of its possibilities that the misused expression 'enjoy yourself,' came into being.

The more you enjoy *yourself*, the more of a person you are.

CASES

Case XV: Miss W. – Miss W. is twenty-seven and has a good secretarial position, with the usual limited salary. She has, also, the Domestic Instinct. So she found herself a so-called one-room apartment – which had, in reality, a not-very-large living-room, a diminutive foyer, a kitchenette the size of a broom-closet, two real closets, and a bath. Its special feature was that it was high up (in a walk-up apartment), and most of two sides of the room were taken up by windows. Miss W. then hunted up a good but inexpensive carpenter and annexed, in addition, another willing worker in the shape of an ardent beau. Under her direction, they constructed in all of the available space on the windowed sides, book-shelves and cupboards made of light colored, modernistic-looking wood. The doors of these conceal a radio, a bar, and a wide variety of shelves and equipment, all as compact as a Pullman. The room contains a couch (also modern, and beige upholstered), which can be turned into a bed; enough, but not too many modern chairs and tables; several white-shaded lamps, and some charming white pottery.

Closets, kitchen, and cupboards contain everything she needs – from Basque linen from Macy's to red glass from the ten-cent store. And the result, while not elegant, is as gay and chic as a millionaire's villa on the Riviera – so charming, in fact, that the beau (now a husband) is sharing it with her, thereby putting Miss W. out of this book.

Case XVI: Miss D. – Miss D. is the same age as Miss W. and has the same salary, but the Domestic Instinct is missing. She doesn't believe in spending money on things that don't show, so she lives in a small, inexpensive room in a boarding-house. It contains a lumpy bed, an ugly bureau, an oak table, and two chairs, and there is a stain in the ceiling from a winter-before-last's leak. Miss D. says it doesn't matter, as she lives her life outside.

When Miss D. leaves for the office at quarter to nine in the morning, or for a date at seven-fifteen or eight-thirty in the evening, she is a work of art, from her beautifully made-up face to her small French heels. But, like the rest of us, she has neither the strength, money, or invitations to go out seven nights a week, and there are also Saturdays, Sundays, and holidays, when she does not go to the office and her hours spent at home are distinctly depressing. When she is sick in bed, she is miserable. The bed is not comfortable enough to encourage sleep, the light is not good enough for reading, and the appearance is not suitable for inviting guests.

Since Miss D. cannot afford to do much entertaining in the smart restaurants where she likes to eat, she is seeing more of the rich friends who invite her to them and less of old friends who do not, and getting to be a bit of a sponger. And since she cannot ask her men friends to her house, she is getting to be a little too ready to go to their apartments. We fear that Miss D. will come to no good end.

Case XVII: Mrs. E. – Mrs. E. is sixty-odd and a widow with five grown children and a very small income. Four of her children are married, and the fifth (a daughter) is a successful decorator in Boston, and all have urged her to live with them. Mrs. E., however, recognizes the voice of duty when she hears it, and does not find it alluring. Moreover, she does not enjoy – for any length of time – her oldest daughter's husband, her youngest daughter's mode of living, her oldest daughter-in-law's housekeeping, or the noise made by the grandchildren in the other two households. She has, therefore, remodeled what was once the gardener's cottage on her most prosperous son's place, and furnished it with what she likes best of the possessions acquired in forty years of married life – regardless of whether or not her decorator-daughter approves of them. She has a garden in which she takes great pleasure; she is delighted that her family and friends come to see her so often; and she goes to see *them* so seldom that her visits are an Occasion.

Case XVIII: Miss F. – Miss F. works in a pattern company and has a good enough position so that everybody wonders why she wears nondescript clothes and commutes from midtown New York to an inaccessible point outside of Yonkers. Her business associates believe that she cherishes an unrequited love, since Miss F. (who is both handsome and intelligent) once lived at a convenient apartment hotel and dressed as well as the best of them.

What they do not know is that Miss F. has always regarded a home as synonymous with Heaven and, for a long time, thought it equally unattainable – since, to Miss F., a home means neither a hotel room nor an apartment. But one day, motoring with a friend, Miss F. came upon an unused carriage-house in the country, apparently unconnected with any estate. (She later discovered that the house had burned down.) There were rambler roses at one end and lilac bushes in front, and Miss F.'s professional enamel of efficiency melted away. She took most of her earnings to buy the place, and the rest of them to remodel it and insure it.

Her dissipations are now in second-hand stores instead of theaters and restaurants, and her extravagances are now in curtains and cutlery instead of spring suits. People often remark (though not to Miss F.) that it is a pity she is letting herself go. This, however, is doing her an injustice. She doesn't neglect her complexion, and her health and figure have been improved by raking and gardening. As to clothes – one wonders if a visit to Miss F.'s house, with English chintz at the windows, bittersweet in copper bowls, and a view of the valley from the flagstone terrace, would not convince her critics that she is getting more than they for her money.

CHAPTER SEVEN

PLEASURES
OF A SINGLE BED

IT IS probably true that most people have more fun in bed than anywhere else, and we are not being vulgar. Even going to bed alone can be alluring. There are many times, in fact, when it's by far the most alluring way to go.

Whether you agree with this or not, you have to go to bed at least once every twenty-four hours, and you will have to keep right on going as long as you live. If you read the statistics, you will find that you spend such a large proportion of your life lying down that it scarcely seems worth the trouble to get up at all. All of which makes it pretty obvious that you might as well make an art of going to bed.

We are all for as much glamour as possible in the bedroom. The single bedroom, as well as the double one. If even the most respectable spinsters would regard their bedrooms as places where anything might happen, the resulting effects would be extremely beneficial.

You may have a small bedroom, or a not very elegant one, but you must have a bed. Make it as good a bed as you can possibly afford. Make it, also, as beautiful as possible. If you can't go in for a modern mirrored bed, or an old mahogany four-poster, or a good reproduction of some other type – then take the bed you have and have the head and foot cut off and a really charming cover made to fit it. With plenty of pillows and your best nightgown, you can be as seductive in this as in any other.

The chief other properties for a successful bedroom scene are a bedside table with a good light for reading, a clock, and a telephone within reach. And it's not a bad idea to have the dressing-table mirror, or some other mirror, hanging directly opposite the foot of the bed, so that you can see yourself when you sit up. This is sometimes depressing, but it acts as a prompter when you feel yourself slipping.

Every woman should work out her own special ritual to be performed religiously every night before getting into bed. And every night does not except those nights when you are dead-tired. Even then, at least a few good strokes with a hair-brush stiff enough to start up circulation, a bit of cuticle oil and a lotion on the hands, cleansing cream and whatever other cream does the most for your face, are just as important as brushing your teeth. On nights when you're home and not so tired, give yourself all the other little personal touches that you need. This is particularly advisable if you don't want to keep on going to bed alone for the rest of your life, but you'd better do it, anyway.

One would naturally suppose that women living alone would be most conscientious about this – from the mere standpoint of convenience. But this doesn't seem to be the case. Perhaps that's why many of them live alone. At any rate, there are hundreds who don't know the difference between a cleansing cream and an emollient – which to our minds is practically the same as being illiterate. With the dust-filled air and hard water of most American cities, no schoolgirl complexion can survive alone and unaided, and it's only intelligent to find out what your own skin needs and apply it. You'll be a better woman if you do.

We would also like to say a few words about your bedroom wardrobe. This is no place to be grim and practical. Don't worry about whether your night-gowns will wear if you are sure that they will flatter. We can think of nothing more depressing than going to bed in a washed-out four-year-old nightgown, nothing more bolstering to the morale than going to bed all fragrant with toilet-water and wearing a luscious pink satin nightgown, well-cut and trailing.

Next, of course, you'll need négligées — at least two, one warm and one thin, and as many more as you can afford. Have them tailored or *chi-chi* according to your type, but have them becoming. And don't think that four bed-jackets are too many if you belong to the breakfast-in-bed school. A warm comfortable one for every-day use and a warm grand one for special occasions. A sheer cool one for summer mornings, and a lacy affair to dress up in. You can make the last two yourself out of remnants, in practically no time at all. For the others, have one of quilted silk or Shetland wool, and another of padded satin or velvet in the shade that makes you most beautiful.

Breakfast in bed is, of course, one of the major delights of living, and we plan to say a great deal more about it in a later chapter on food. There is no more rejuvenating habit, also, than having dinner in bed when you're tired. If you're very tired, have only a bowl of steaming hot soup, and perhaps some fruit-juice just before you go to sleep. If you're fighting a cold, have a glass of fruit-juice instead of the soup, and, before you turn off the light, some hot lemonade or a hot toddy. If you're bothered by insomnia, try Bovril, or hot milk, or camomile tea as your nightcap.

In any case, look upon the evening as a party. Even if you've never liked staying in bed – we've heard that there are people like this – persuade yourself that it's fun and keep at it till it actually is. Plan what you're going to do in advance, and have all the requisites at hand – a good book, or some new magazines, or the things you need for writing letters. And make yourself very, very comfortable, as well as as handsome as you know how.

All this applies if you're really sick and spending a whole day in bed. In this case, try to have a maid

and luxuriate in being waited on. If this is impossible, plan your day when you first wake up, so
that you will get up only occasionally, and when you
are up collect the things you are likely to need in the
next few hours, instead of hopping out of bed for a
pencil or a nail-file every few minutes. (Speaking of
nail-files – a day in bed is a perfect chance to soak
your nails in hot olive-oil and give them a little
special care afterward.) Unless you are very, very sick,
the advice to fix yourself up holds good. If you can't
do this, send for the doctor.

Incidentally, don't stay alone if you are very sick.
Go to a hospital or to a relative's house. You'll be
better off in a small hospital ward (these can be very
comfortable indeed) if that is the only alternative to
staying in your own room with no one to look out for
you. When you are ill is *not* the time to be noble and
often it is not the time to show your spunk. Spunk
may be a virtue when you're in good health, but it
can be a vice when you're sick. The sensible thing is
to go in for being a weak woman thoroughly and
intelligently and get over your complaint as rapidly
as possible.

If you are new at the game of living alone, it is not
unlikely that you are sometimes afraid of the dark,

though, of course, you don't admit it. This, too, is something to get over quickly; you can have a miserable time prolonging the agony. When you wake up in the night convinced that you hear a man moving about in the next room, do *not* get up and investigate. Still more important, do *not* telephone the janitor, or a friend's husband across the street, or your brother in New Jersey. Almost certainly, there is no man in the next room, and, if there were, he would be gone by the time anyone got there. The trick is to turn over and think furiously about something else, like your new dress or what you'd say if the good-looking man who took you to the theater last week proposed – until you go to sleep again. This is difficult at first, but after the sixth imaginary burglar has invaded your flat unmolested, it becomes no trouble at all.

If all this sounds a little dreary, think of the things that you, all alone, don't have to do. You don't have to turn out your light when you want to read, because somebody else wants to sleep. You don't have to have the light on when you want to sleep, because somebody else wants to read. You don't have to get up in the night to fix somebody else's hot-water bottle, or lie awake listening to snores, or be vivacious when you're tired, or cheerful when you're blue, or sympathetic when you're bored. You probably have your bathroom all to yourself, too, which is unquestionably one of Life's Great Blessings. You don't have to wait till someone finishes shaving, when you are all set for a cold-cream session. You have no one complaining about your pet bottles, no one to drop wet towels on the floor, no one occupying the bathtub when you have just time to take a shower. From dusk until dawn, you can do exactly as you please, which, after all, is a pretty good allotment in this world where a lot of conforming is expected of everyone.

CASES

Case XIX: Miss P. – Miss P. is a young lady of limited income, but unlimited ingenuity. She has a two-room apartment in Washington, which is a charming setting for her blonde beauty and which she uses to advantage. Unfortunately, the upkeep takes so much of Miss P.'s salary that she frequently finds herself in embarrassing situations, but she believes the results are worth the difficulty.

Recently, an old school friend who lives in Chicago came to Washington for a two-days' visit. It was plainly Miss P.'s duty to entertain her in a manner quite beyond the momentary ability of her pocketbook. She was, also, a lady whom Miss P. wanted to impress, in return for a few high-hattings of boarding-school days. Miss P., therefore, considered her resources carefully, turned the matter over in her mind, and – the lady's visit occurring over a week-end – took to her bed.

From that vantage-point, she telephoned an effusive invitation. 'I'm desolate,' she said, 'that I can't show you the town.' (And so she was.) 'But do be an angel and come and have tea with me. I'm in bed, but not a bit contagious.'

When the guest arrived, she was ushered into Miss P.'s bedroom, in which the late afternoon sun filtered through white Venetian blinds and fell upon a bowl of roses on a low mirrored table. Miss P. herself, perfectly groomed, was propped against pillows, wearing an opalescent white satin nightgown with Alençon lace and a shell-pink velvet bed-jacket. The blanket cover on her bed was shell-pink, too, with strips of lace.

During tea, which was impeccably served by a colored maid-in-for-the-afternoon, Miss P. was twice called on the telephone by beaux. This was a coincidence arranged by Miss P. only through great ingenuity.

When the guest left, practically wilted with envy, Miss P. reflected that the total expenditure had been two dollars for the maid, one dollar for the roses, and a very little extra for the tea — a well-spent investment and a great deal less than taxis, cocktails, and lunch in a restaurant — the least she would have felt that she could do out of bed.

Miss P., incidentally, had a good rest.

Case XX: Mrs. O. — Mrs. O. is middle-aged, outspoken, energetic, and divorced. She wears mannish tailleurs and is active in women's clubs and the movement to promote birth control. She refers with scorn to women who are kitchen-minded, and it is evident in her own apartment that her contempt spills over into living-room, bedroom, and bath. While the rooms are not actually uncomfortable, they are so dull as to be depressing, and there is nothing in them that you would want.

Mrs. O.'s bedroom contains a cot bed with a blue denim cover, a high mahogany veneer bureau, a black-painted bookcase, a wicker chair, a table holding a student lamp and a china tray with a safety-pin, some hairpins, and a collection of odd buttons, two faded rag rugs, bargain net curtains, and reproductions of Saint Cecilia and Rosa Bonheur's *The Fair* on the walls.

Mrs. O. (quite understandably) never spent much time there until, not long ago, her numerous activities caused a near-nervous breakdown, and the doctor ordered her to go to bed every night before dinner and to stay in bed over the week-ends. Threats of a sanatorium caused Mrs. O. to obey.

Never having developed any ability for graceful living at home, Mrs. O.'s evenings and week-ends are not successes. By noon, she begins to dread the end of the day, and she comes home in a distinctly

disgruntled mood. She puts on an unbecoming rayon nightgown (Mrs. O. believes in economizing in the bedroom and buys nightgowns that needn't be ironed) and a dark blue corduroy bathrobe (which doesn't soil) and gets into her uninviting bed. Having claimed that she detested eating in bed for the last forty years, she stews all the time her dinner-tray is in her lap – which causes her badly trained maid to feel that it's not worth while to bother much about dinner, anyway. Since the light is badly arranged for reading and Mrs. O. has no ingenuity about doing anything else in bed, she spends most of the evening thrashing around resentfully, getting the bed mussed up and the bathrobe into uncomfortable rolls.

When Mrs. O.'s friends drop in to see her they leave wondering whether she is so efficient after all. Several of them have also thought that perhaps it was *not* so surprising that, ten years or so ago, Mr. O. ran off with his pretty stenographer.

CHAPTER EIGHT

WILL YOU
OR WON'T YOU?

QUESTION: Is it true that the attitude towards the morals of women on their own has changed so much in the last twenty years that it is no longer considered wrong for an unattached woman to have an affair? That is, do really nice women have them?

Answer: If you are hoping that we are going to tell you to go as far as you like, so that the responsibility won't be on your shoulders, you are in for a disappointment. This is every woman's own special problem, which nobody else can settle.

The one thing your best friend really won't tell you is whether or not she is what was once known as a Good Woman. There is nothing about which people are so voluble as chastity applied to the other person, or so reticent as chastity applied to themselves. Whether or not a woman has had her Moments, if she has a grain of common sense she keeps it to herself, since, if she has, most people would be shocked, and, if she hasn't, the rest would be superior.

It would be foolish to pretend that things are as they used to be, however. A Woman's Honor is no longer mentioned with bated breath and protected by her father, her brother, and the community. It is now her own affair.

If you were to base the answer to your question on current literature, it would be Yes – practically every woman on her own goes in for one affair, at least. If you were to base it on cases you actually know, it would be, 'No – no nice woman ever does.' You would be wrong, either way.

So many volumes have been written on the Sex Life of the Unmarried Woman in the last twenty years, and so many thousand cases listed, that if you waded through them you would emerge feeling that you were the sole surviving virgin. This, too, would be far from the truth. Until recently, the burden of the song was that a little sex life wasn't such a bad idea. Lately, the tune has changed – investigation over a longer period of years having, apparently, caused the startling discovery that the Woman Pays.

As you are probably used to paying for everything from the rent to your own pearls, we don't expect this statement to stop you from having your fling. What you probably want to know is: How much does she pay? And is it worth it? She pays, as a matter of fact, in a great many ways – in a thousand little shabbinesses and humiliations, in the almost inevitable bitter ending, and in nervous wear and tear. She also, if she's wise, goes right on paying her own personal expenses.

Living alone, she has, of course, one advantage over other women – but also one added temptation – a lack of privacy being more responsible for upholding the morals of the nation than anything short of the Bible. No minister, doctor, or scientist has ever had the restraining influence of a good healthy fear that Father or Older Sister might barge in.

Certainly, affairs should not even be thought of before you are thirty. Once you have reached this age, if you will not hurt any third person and can take all that you will have to take – take it silently, with dignity, with a little humor, and without any weeping or wailing or gnashing of teeth – perhaps the experience will be worth it to you. Or perhaps it won't.

The sad truth is that whatever you decide, you'll think you regret it. You'll hate the shabby end of romance, and you'll detest missing it altogether.

If there's any answer, it is probably to walk a straight and narrow path, keeping so busy and amused that you haven't time to stew about the things you lack. Keeping also – and this is the best trick we know of – enough men and mystery about you so that nobody can guess how you have solved the problem.

Question: May a lady living alone with her maid, in an apartment with a guest-room, occasionally invite a man friend to spend the night, if he comes from out of town and is a very old friend or distant relative?

Answer: It all depends on what is worrying you. If it's what the neighbors will say, invite him by all means and let them say it. Gossip, while still a favorite form of conversation, is treated less and less seriously and deserves to be snubbed. If you are worried about the gentleman's behavior, that is another matter. You probably know him better than we do, but it is our opinion that it usually takes two to make a situation.

Question: Is there any reason why a woman should not entertain her men friends at dinner occasionally and invite them to be her escorts when she has theater or concert tickets? Must she always wait for a man to return her courtesy before inviting him a second time?

Answer: There is not the slightest reason why a woman should not invite a man to dinner or to go with her to the theater or a concert. How often she can ask him depends on several things – primarily, whether or not she has designs on him, and if so, what they are.

The old school will, of course, regard practically everything you do as pursuit. Some men like it; some don't. You needn't worry too much about it, as you are probably not risking this on a man whom you would like to have around permanently. However, as no man will believe that you could have this negative attitude towards him, and most of them will be wary accordingly, it's a good idea to exercise a reasonable caution on them all. An assortment of presentable escorts is a great convenience.

There is no denying that you can be a lot more aggressive now than you could have been a few years ago. Things that are taken for granted today would have made you a hussy then. This was due at first to economic conditions (blamed for everything nowadays), which prevented so many young men from getting around much that stag-lines dwindled, until it began to be quite usual for the girls to pay for practically everything. It being human nature for most people to take all that they can get, this state

of affairs was soon taken for granted — although there are still a few chivalrous gentlemen who believe that the man should be the provider.

There are, also, a few women who will tell you that most men are spoiled and that, as far as they are concerned, a man will have to pay the bills or stay away. These women are usually the sirens, as the others find that the men do stay away. After all, it's better to be brazen than neglected.

The best rule is to make your invitations worth accepting and not to care what the man thinks so long as he comes. As to how often you can ask him successfully — that must be decided according to every individual case. How well do you know him? How willing a victim is he? Could he afford to do better by you? Hold a little mental investigation of the case — and then do exactly as you please.

CHAPTER NINE

A LADY AND HER LIQUOR

PRACTICALLY anybody old enough to read these words can remember when few, if any, ladies drank. Feminine lips that touched whisky were, of course, almost unmentionable, whisky being definitely a man's drink. As for a woman who lived alone and kept liquor in her cupboard – she was referred to in hushed tones as a woman with an affliction, like insanity or epilepsy.

Today, the woman who doesn't drink is more apt to have high blood-pressure than moral prejudices.

In even the most feminine restaurants, where men are rare (and uninteresting), the majority of customers take cocktails, and as many whisky drinks as gin drinks are sold. In feminine apartments, as a rule, not even the occasional teetotaler begrudges a highball to a guest. Enjoying your friends' drinks, but never serving any, seems like another form of sponging, and most people feel that they are boring when they don't drink with the crowd.

But for all this modern viewpoint, there are plenty of ladies who don't seem to know very much about liquor. You see them in bars, looking vague when their escorts ask them what they want; you hear them in restaurants, murmuring vaguely that they'd like 'one of those pale drinks with olives in them.' They accept meekly the masculine assumption that it's the men who know all about liquor, and we hate to think what they may put into their crystal cocktail shakers at home.

But why should men be the only ones to know their drinks? If you're going to serve them, as apparently you are, why not serve the right ones at the right time and know how to mix them? It's not an asset to be known as that woman who serves the terrible apple-jack cocktails.

We are not urging you to serve any liquor at all. We are not going into the matter of morals — which is, after all, nobody's business but your own. But whatever your ideas on the subject, it's very useful to know the ABCs of drinking. Even if you never drink, but more especially if you do, understanding what to drink and how much is pretty important. And understanding what to serve and when is invaluable to any hostess.

There is no simpler way of entertaining successfully than having a cocktail party, and there is no surer way of making a casual guest have a good time, than serving a highball. For breaking ice, mixing strangers, and increasing popularity, alcohol is still unrivaled, Mrs. Boole and all her willing workers to the contrary.

Fortunately, it is entirely possible to have occasional cocktail parties and to keep on hand an adequate supply of the necessary ingredients for drinks to serve unexpectedly, all without having a cellar. With seven bottles and a small amount of knowledge, anybody can be a good hostess.

As a surprising number of women lack even this knowledge, we will start from the beginning. The seven essential bottles contain sherry, gin, Scotch, rye, French and Italian vermouth, and bitters. Sherry for the mild drinkers and more and more for the sophisticated ones. Gin and both vermouths for Martinis. Scotch for highballs; rye and bitters for the Old-Fashioneds, and rye, bitters, and Italian vermouth for Manhattans. All of these things can be used in dozens of other ways, of course, and you can add innumerable bottles, but you can get just as far with these seven. You can, in fact, go too far with even fewer. If you are a beginner as a bartender, we advise you to stick to these and leave the drinks with the fancy names and the fancy colors to the professionals.

Buying liquor may seem like a problem in itself, but, in reality, it has ceased to be one of the great masculine mysteries. Like so many of them, it turns out to be a simple matter after all. All you really need to do is to go to a reliable shop and get confidential with the salesman. Tell him any doubts in your mind and watch him respond chivalrously to a lady in distress. He will like it, and you will come out with as satisfactory a purchase as though your most hard-drinking friend had bought it. You may feel a little silly, but it is better to be silly than stung.

If you go into a not-so-reliable shop, you will probably be sold a bargain, and bargains in liquor, like bargains in clothes, are only for Those Who Know. While you are still learning, never buy anything but the best. (This is not a bad rule to stick to through life.)

If you don't want to leave it to the salesman, ask a friend who serves good cocktails to tell you the names of one or two good brands of each kind of liquor and memorize them. If the shop you go to hasn't got them, go to another shop. Incidentally, buy an imported sherry that came from Spain by way of England. It's an old Spanish custom to embroider the truth on labels, but British reserve holds true here as elsewhere. And get fairly dry sherry, but not the dryest. Very dry sherry is something that most people drink because they have heard it was chic and not because they like it.

Having bought the ingredients, there is still the matter of mixing them. One of the ABCs here is to know that whisky or gin (or rum) is the alcoholic base of most mixed drinks and that a jigger is an average amount for each drink. (A dash extra is sometimes a good idea and sometimes not; but skimping will never make you popular.) Remember, too, never, never to mix Scotch with anything but plain or charged water.

As to the recipes, you can, of course, get a good book and follow it. But anybody ought to be able to master the recipes for Martinis, Manhattans, and Old-Fashioneds without undue strain. Having mastered them, do not try to improve on them. You can't. This is not a field in which to use your imagination. Don't think, either, that it would be nice to have some unfamiliar cocktail for variety. Your guests won't agree with you. Worse, even, than the woman who puts marshmallows in a salad is the one who goes in for fancy cocktails.

Here are some standard recipes for the drinks we've suggested.

Highballs: a jigger of Scotch in a tall glass with ice and plain or charged water. Or a jigger of rye, with ice and ginger-ale or charged water.

Martinis: two parts gin to one-half part French and one-half part Italian vermouth. Add a twist of lemon-peel and ice and stir (not shake) till really cold. Serve with a pitted, unstuffed olive in each glass. (There are innumerable variations of this recipe, but this one is a classic.)

Old-Fashioneds: Set out one glass for each person.

Place a lump of sugar in each glass, add a dash of Angostura bitters and a very little water and crush the sugar. Put in each glass a slice of orange, a slice of lemon, a stick of fresh pineapple, and a maraschino cherry. Add a jigger of rye and fill the glass with ice. Serve a 'muddler' with each glass and let your guests amuse themselves.

Manhattans: Two parts rye to one part Italian vermouth and a dash of Angostura bitters. Add ice and shake and serve with a cherry in each glass. (A cherry with a stem is an epicurian touch.)

One of these four drinks is almost everybody's favorite, but you will have occasional guests with violent theories about what is good for them (and you). The two largest schools are the No-Sugar-with-Alcohol School and the Never-Mix-Fruit-Juice-and-Alcohol School. Leave out the sugar in Old-Fashioneds for the first, and don't serve Old-Fashioneds to the second. For all the other drink dieters, Scotch and soda or Scotch and plain water is the answer.

Above all, don't serve fruit-juice and gin cocktails indiscriminately. These are responsible for most of those Mornings After.

Serve the sherry and the cocktails before meals,

the highballs after or between meals. And don't worry about what to serve *with* meals. In spite of reams of literature on the subject, comparatively little wine is served at American tables, and what does appear is apt to be a mistake. We are practically an illiterate nation in the matter of wines and when and how to serve them; and there is very little use in educating yourself, as almost nobody will know that you're doing right anyway. Besides, the cocktails that most of your guests will want make further drinking a superfluity, if not a catastrophe.

Every woman soon works out her own idea on what to serve to whom, but – in general – most women like sherry, and this is, of course, the easiest, since it demands no preliminaries. It has the added advantage of being better for you – or, at least, less bad for you – than most drinks, and it is so impeccably correct that you can easily make any guest feel that she ought to like it, if she doesn't. Martinis are the cheapest of the drinks recommended and popular enough so that you can serve them to anyone unblushingly. Old-Fashioneds come into the economy class after a fashion, because of the fact that you make them singly, and usually people don't expect two. Leave the other drinks to the people you want to have settle down and stay. Scotch (or rye) and contentment are practically synonymous.

Equipment is important, too, and this is a place where feminine fanciness is out of place, but prevalent. Have good plain glass shakers, with a special one (or a special top) for stirring the Martinis instead of shaking them. Have a jigger and use it. Good cocktails are seldom made by guesswork. Have a wooden muddler to crush the sugar in Old-Fashioneds, and a shaker top on the bitters bottle. And have simple, sturdy glasses of the standard types and a large, firm tray that doesn't show rings.

Before discussing the accompaniments to cocktails, let us get into a corner and whisper a word or two about the effects. Not so long ago, no lady would have admitted that she felt any. Drunkenness then, as now, was revolting, and you were either drunk or sober. Now it is granted that even a perfect lady is occasionally somewhere between the two, with a definite leaning, of course, towards sober. Nor is this condemned as it once was. There are those who feel that there is no pleasanter feeling than that moment when you arrive at the dinner-table, heaven knows how, and are aware that everything beyond the table is vague, like a semilighted stage-set, while the shirt-fronts of the men and the white shoulders and jewels of the women are more acutely accented than ever before. But this is an experience for a lady who understands fine shadings. For the next step is neither charming nor attractive. Sensations that you keep to yourself are all very well, but shrill voices, familiarities, vulgar stories, and other obvious results of a lack of discretion are, frankly, disgusting.

Having completed that little sermon, let us turn to the question of what goes with the drinks. There are two schools of thought about this. There is the drinks-with-no-food school, followed by heavy drinkers and a few sophisticates and dyspeptics, and the much bigger school that regards the accompanying tidbits as half of the party. The latter is responsible for an infinite variety of delicacies and horrors to serve with cocktails.

You can take your choice, but here are a few suggestions.

First of all, in a ménage-for-one, simplification is usually important – and here is an ideal place for it. Cocktail accompaniments should be appetizers, and not a large part of the meal. They should never have a hint of sweetness, with the one possible exception of a plain, very thin, slightly sweetened biscuit served with sherry. They should not be too fancy, or too varied, since the accompanying liquids are apt to increase the appetite and decrease the discretion.

It's all very well to serve elaborate canapés at a grand party, but you probably don't give many grand parties. Small, informal ones are more fun and much easier, especially if you haven't much space or service. And at these, elaborate canapés seem a bit pretentious. Try, instead, a bowl of huge, well-chilled olives and some crisp, salty, unsweetened crackers spread with fish and cheese mixtures. Or two or three varieties of the really good cheese biscuits, such as twiglets, cheddar and piquant sandwiches, and Chantilly crackers. (There are some dull ones, too, which would justify any discriminating guest in talking about you behind your back.) And perhaps salted nuts or cheese popcorn.

Whatever you do, don't let the cocktail hour be a burden. Its purpose in life is to inject a little gaiety into a weary world, and, if it doesn't do that for you, you might as well get your fun out of wearing a white ribbon and making soap-box speeches for the W.C.T.U.

CASES

Case XXI: Mrs. A. – Mrs. A. is a young divorcée who feels very bitter about the blow Fate has dealt her. She is, also, supersensitive about the manlessness of her ménage. She endeavors to make up for it in various unnecessary ways, one of which is an insistence on three rounds of cocktails when she entertains.

Her friends (like herself) are not heavy drinkers. They do not want three cocktails. But they get them and – just as you would – they drink them. Mrs. A.'s dinners have been known to chill while the last shaker was emptied. By then, the guests were beyond being critical, but also beyond being appreciative, which is a pity, as Mrs. A. serves excellent dinners. Some of her most attractive guests, who have had some bad Mornings-After as a result of Mrs. A.'s entertainment, now have previous engagements when she phones her invitations.

Case XXII: Miss C. – Miss C. is an extremely ambitious young woman in her early thirties, who cannot take much time from her work for housekeeping. She therefore lives in a two-room non-housekeeping apartment and eats most of her meals in restaurants. This is all very well till it comes to the matter of entertaining, when she cannot deny that there's no place like home. Being ingenious, however, she has worked out her own little scheme, which copes with the No-Ice Problem.

Miss C. has arranged her own version of a bar on a shelf in the closet off the living-room. The shelf is edged with engaging red, white, and blue plaid pleating. On it, you will find a charming red Bohemian glass decanter and sherry glasses, a group of crystal plates and small dishes, several bottles of sherry, one bottle of *glüg*, a box containing small glass knives with red glass handles, three or four small jars of 'spreads' (such as Roquefort, anchovy, and pimento), a box of unsweetened crackers, and a supply of cocktail napkins. At a moment's notice, any or all of these can be transferred to the modern glass coffee-table beside the living-room couch.

The jars of 'spreads' are tiny, since, once opened, they have to be used up or thrown away. They are placed on little glass plates on the table, each with a knife beside it, and the guests roll their own. This furnishes entertainment and conversation, as well as saving labor. As Miss C. cannot go in for cocktails, without ice, she has made a specialty of sherry, hunting up the best and keeping several varieties on hand. The *glüg*, a delicious Swedish drink, hot and powerful, she keeps for guests who look upon sherry as effeminate.

Case XXIII: Mrs. E. – Mrs. E. is an optimistic widow who lives in a Chicago suburb, amid the slightly out-of-date elegance supplied by the late Mr. E. Having heard that the way to a man's heart is through his stomach and verified the statement once, she is now endeavoring to repeat the performance. This time, she is concentrating on drink rather than food, and an unfortunate fondness for things that are

'just a little bit different' is growing upon her. She has a tendency to apply this to her cocktails, and, when she entertains, she extemporizes in the matter of mixing odd bits from the vast array of bottles assembled by Mr. E. The results are startling in both taste and effect.

The neighbors complain of occasional uproars disturbing the nights in the vicinity of Mrs. E.'s house. Her friends are beginning to talk about the run-down look caused by stains and cigarette burns on the furniture, and once, at least, the police have been called to inquire into the commotion.

CHAPTER TEN

THE GREAT UNITER

IT IS all very well to be highbrow, but anyone who thinks that this means having a mind above meals is not quite bright. There is probably nothing that gives as much pleasure as food, not excepting love. Dull food, poor food, and badly served food can undermine your morals, while interesting food can make life seem very pleasant after all.

You have heard this said since your first dish of prunes, but, if you live alone, it probably slips your mind from time to time. There is no denying that it

107

is hard to make meals for one only seem worth the effort. Solitary meals, also, are a comfortably inconspicuous place to economize. But this is the wrong place, my children; you can't be great strong girls without plenty of nourishment. And there is seldom the right sort of nourishment in a meal 'out of the ice-box.'

Having three square meals a day is not enough – they ought to be three meals that you get a kick out of. We'll begin with breakfast, which, in too many houses, is as dull as a meal at Sing Sing.

We might as well assume to start with that breakfast is the meal at which you consider your figure. Very well, then, have your orange-juice and black coffee and toast. We are not urging chicken livers or waffles with sausages and syrup, though they do make a pleasant change now and then. Our plea is merely for plenty of orange-juice, coffee, and toast; really good orange-juice, coffee, and toast; and orange-juice, coffee, and toast attractively served.

Of course, the civilized place for any woman to have breakfast is in bed. We might except Mother on the Farm, or the Italian lady whose family took the prize for size at the Chicago Fair. But for you and me, who live alone and whose early mornings are uncomplicated by offspring, farm-hands, and even husbands, bed is the place. (There is, of course, the chance that you are one of those who fling back the covers and spring lightly out of bed with a song on your lips in the early morning – but, in that case, you will have flung this book out of the window with something very different from a song long before this.)

The breakfast tray is not so difficult, even if you get your own breakfast and have to be at the office at nine. In any case, you have to get up for your shower – and it's a good idea, while you're at it, to comb your hair and put on powder and lipstick. This being done, it's endurable – if not enticing – to wend your way into the kitchen and go domestic. We are not recommending this as a lark, but it can be borne. The trick is to work out a system by which you can attain a glass – a large and good-looking glass (none of those dinky 'orange-juice' affairs) – full of ice-cold orange-juice, a pot of good, steaming hot coffee, hot toast made according to your own pet notions, a little marmalade or honey thrown in, and all of it arranged on a tray with some gay color scheme. Yellow is nice, with amber glass for your orange-juice, or a breakfast set of flowered English china, or an all-white Wedgwood set on bright colored linen.

All we ask is that you *don't* fill your tray with a mixed-up collection of odds and ends.

Maybe you think you're ready to go back to bed and eat your breakfast now – but are the pillows plumped up freshly and is your very best bed-jacket ready? And what about the morning paper? Perhaps you stand on your feet all day in a none too impressive job – be an elegant lady of leisure just the same, from, say, seven-forty-five to eight-fifteen. Even though nobody knows, you'll be more of a person the rest of the day.

Skipping over lunch hastily, as most of us do, we arrive at dinner, and we can't say too much about dinner in the grand manner for a woman by herself. Not a pompous meal at a lonely dining-room table, like a *grande dame* of the nineties, but dinner at a little table beside the fire, or dinner on the chaise longue, or dinner in bed, or dinner on a balcony – or any place else that is comfortable and attractive. Dress up a bit for it. Here is the perfect place for a trailing négligée and frou-frou. The woman who always looks at night as though she were expecting a suitor is likely to have several. (One of the pleasantest things about modern life is the increased span of beaux.)

THE GREAT UNITER

Among the problems for the diner-alone is the dread of left-overs. They are all very well once, but we feel no enthusiasm ourselves for seventh-day chicken. Yet a little ingenuity can overcome this, with no fear of monotony. Lots of good things to eat come in small packages.

We are not going into the matter of menus, which you can find in any magazine or newspaper. But just to prove our point, here are a few dishes that won't hang on and on. First, of course, the old familiar lamb-chop, or any other kind of chop. There are also chicken livers or calf's liver, which you can buy in small quantities and serve with its partner, bacon. There are sweetbreads, and squabs for days when you feel like being elegant. There is corned-beef, which you can buy in one thick slice at the delicatessen store and make into delectable hash. There are very small pork tenderloins, which are specially good boiled first, then baked with canned peaches.

Then the good books (on things to eat) tell us that we don't eat half enough fish — which is a perfect solution for the small purchaser. Crab-meat, lobster meat, scallops, fillet of sole, and a variety of other fish can be bought in as small quantities as you please. So can mushrooms – delectable when creamed and baked. And what about eggs baked in ramekins with cheese, or eggs Benedict, or eggs à la king, or scrambled eggs with tomatoes or perhaps asparagus?

Any of these as a basis, with soup, a vegetable, and some green salad with French dressing and a little cheese, makes a dinner at which you wouldn't mind having your worst friend drop in. Or you might substitute fruit for the salad – melon or chilled berries or a compote. (A very special one combines big black cherries, which you can get in cans, with canned pears. And did you ever try fresh peaches with raspberry sauce over them?)

Though you may have no maid and are definitely anti-domestic, things are not hopeless. There is the great army of canned things – and we don't mean just tomato soup and green peas. We mean shad roe, and green turtle soup, for instance, and a great many other things, too. The possibilities in canned soup alone will make you famous as a cook. And lots of the cans now come in one-woman size.

There are, also, the Exchanges for Woman's Work, dotted all over the country, at which all sorts of home-cooking delicacies are sold, and more other places to help you meet your problem that we can name. There are even firms that will deliver your dinner all hot and steaming, at the moment you want it, though we don't know how.

Entertaining in a small ménage is more difficult, but don't be discouraged, for it's worth the effort. Cocktails are, of course, the easiest means, and we've had our say about them. Bridge comes next, and food to go with it should be simple. Highballs, perhaps, and sandwiches. Or beer and crackers and cheese. In this case, have two or three varieties of cheese, such as Bel Paese and Camembert, Cheddar in port, and perhaps Roquefort. Serve them on a cheese-board with a cheese-knife, and have crisp salted crackers as an accompaniment. If you have just one table of players, it's easiest to serve your refreshments after the game, but, if there are several tables, you might have all of the food arranged on a side-table, and let people help themselves whenever one of them is dummy.

If you're a lady of leisure, there is always tea. We really mean tea, too. Serve it with elegance, from a silver tea-set, if you have one, or from a fine china one. With it, serve only paper-thin sandwiches, with watercress in them, perhaps, or sliced cucumber. Or you might serve infinitesimal hot biscuits, with or without marmalade. Or small strips of cinnamon toast. We will not insult your intelligence by warning against rich frosted layer-cakes or – heaven forbid – ice-cream!

If your social debts are mounting, a buffet supper is the answer. You'll be surprised to find what a lot of people you can feed in a very little space. But don't think there aren't pitfalls. A poorly planned buffet supper can be worse than a meal in a cheap cafeteria.

To begin with, don't expect your guests to balance plates, cups, and glasses in their laps. Few of them will turn out to be prestidigitators, and salad on the floor or coffee down the back helps neither rugs nor dispositions. Card-tables folded inconspicuously against the wall can be whisked out at a moment's notice, or, if you haven't enough of these, use other small tables, cleared previously of what-nots. But have even those out of the way when your guests arrive and during the cocktails, so that your rooms (or room) won't seem crowded at first and guests will be able to move around.

The meal itself needn't be elaborate, but it should be very, very good. None of those chicken-patty-and-Saratoga-chip banalities. If you start with soup, have a very special soup. Have at least one hot dish. A good one is a mixture of noodles, chicken livers, and a tomato sauce flavored with port wine. Newburgs are good choices, too, or a mousse of halibut or salmon. With the mousse have a bowl of tartar sauce, another of horseradish sauce mixed with whipped cream. Or you might serve chicken curry with rice and all the usual little tidbits – chutney, chopped peanuts, Bombay duck, green pepper, coconut, and chopped hard-boiled eggs. If you want a second hot dish, try ham cooked in cider or diced ham and hard-boiled eggs baked in creamed sauce.

If you have two hot dishes, it's fun to have one at each end of your buffet table, served in chafing-dishes, each presided over by one of the guests. And to go with them, a huge bowl of green salad; or of greens mixed with cucumbers, tomatoes, and radishes; or a mixed vegetable salad. You might have, also, a cold beef tongue in jelly, or a platter of deviled eggs. Hot rolls, of course, and chilled olives. For dessert, an ice sent in from a caterer simplifies preparation and pleases everybody. With small cakes and coffee, your meal is complete.

Whether you entertain one guest at a time or several at once, you can build up your reputation as a hostess, not so much by having a lot to eat, as by unexpected dishes. Here is a good place to be sophisticated and even a bit snooty. Hunt up foreign grocers – there are sure to be some, wherever you live – and try some of their delicacies. Greek olives; Armenian fruit compote (with orange-peel and pine-nuts among other things); Russian borsch; Hungarian chestnut purée; Swedish goat cheese; Mexican tamale pie – the list is practically endless, and all of these dishes furnish, not merely nourishment, but excellent conversation. There are few things that people grow more lyrical about than their culinary likes and dislikes.

CASES

Case XXIV: Miss V. – Miss V. lives in a not very imaginative mid-town apartment with living-room, bedroom, kitchen, and bath, but her life there is unimportant, since she is a lady who has allowed her job to dominate her outside interests. Recently, however, her feminine instincts bubbled through the crust of efficiency, and she decided to spend a nice long week-end enjoying domesticity and her own flat. She made no engagements from Saturday noon to Monday morning, but she also made no preparations. Saturday afternoon, she spent in puttering and in preparing a not-too-successful dinner. Sunday morning, she woke up considerably earlier than she expected, not having noted that the Sunday on which you have nothing to do is never the Sunday on which you sleep late. She got up, made a sketchy toilet, and put on something suitable for more puttering around the house. This made her look and feel like something suitable for more puttering around the house. She then prepared a casual and uninspired breakfast, which she ate in the kitchen, experiencing a vague dissatisfaction with life in the meantime.

She spent the next two or three hours straightening bureau drawers and closets and reading the morning paper, which did not prove to be much fun. By noon, she felt a little flat. She decided to have some luncheon, but the ice-box proved disappointingly uninteresting. As she was to be alone, she had planned nothing special, and the left-overs made a badly balanced and unappetizing meal.

The 'nice long afternoon to read' proved to be not merely long, but endless. She had taken a book from the library without knowing enough about it, and she found it dull. She took a nap and woke up with her head feeling dull, too. Then she telephoned six friends in rapid succession, but all who were at home had engagements for the rest of the day. By this time, she felt both bored and unpopular. Eventually, she put on her hat and had supper in a restaurant, where the surrounding couples and quartets made her very, very sorry for herself. She went to bed with the firm belief that nobody loved her and business was her only outlet.

Case XXV: Miss R. – Miss R. is a bright young person who puts in a strenuous day in an office, but does not believe in letting her work cut into her social life. At five-thirty she blossoms out, and from then on she has a whirl. Not long ago, however, she decided that she needed a little rest and planned her week-end accordingly.

Directly after lunch on Saturday, she went to a good beauty parlor, where she spent the entire afternoon having a shampoo, a finger-wave, a facial, a manicure, and a pedicure. This was an extravagance, but the shampoo, finger-wave, and manicure were necessities that were included in her budget, and she considered that the other items cost no more than she would ordinarily spend on Saturday shopping and entertainment. This over, she started for home, pausing on the way at the grocer's, where she laid in a supply of her favorite things to eat.

Back in her apartment, she found the cleaning-woman, whom she had arranged to have come late, so that she could stay on and prepare and serve dinner. After giving her direction, Miss R. proceeded to take a tub, first wrapping her head securely in a towel and then adding a generous quantity of bath salts to the water and nourishing cream to her face. She stayed in the tub long enough to relax thoroughly, then rubbed herself down with a pet toilet-water.

After this, she put on a brief step-in and a pair of maroon satin lounging pajamas and ensconced herself on the couch in the living room, armed with two or three of the latest magazines. Before dinner, the maid brought her a glass of sherry and some simple crackers.

Dinner, served on a tray, consisted of a soup-plate (not a cup) of black bean soup with a slice of lemon floating on top; a miniature casserole containing some fresh crab-flakes baked with a cream sauce flavored with sherry and served with some French peas; and endive salad with Roquefort cheese dressing. Coffee was omitted, since the night was to be dedicated to plenty of sleep.

Dinner over, Miss R. spent an hour writing letters and then went to bed. But first, she arranged several cushions comfortably, got out a quilted satin bed-jacket, and put a glass of ice-water on the bedside table. She also had a new novel, by a favorite author. She read till she felt sleepy, then turned out the light.

The next morning, after her shower, Miss R. made up as though she were going out. She then arranged the bed freshly, put the Sunday paper on a chair near by, and prepared her breakfast. For this, the week-day fruit, coffee, toast, and marmalade was augmented by a small coffee-cake and two slices of bacon.

Back in bed (again with the quilted bed-jacket), Miss R. munched contentedly and read the paper — news, scandals, book-reviews, theatrical news, and all, including the obituaries, and enjoying herself thoroughly. When this began to pall, she took up the telephone (within reach of the bed, of course — we said Miss R. was a bright young person) and proceeded to call up several friends. Settled back among the cushions, she had a good satisfying gossip with each, which put her in an excellent frame of mind. Miss R. did not get up until lunch time, when she prepared a tray with the remainder of the black bean soup, an avocado salad, and some Melba toast. After this, she read more of the novel until three-thirty, when she dressed and – hold fast to your seats here – went to church. (Miss R. was brought up by parents who believed that the week went better when it was preceded by church on Sunday, and, in spite of all attempts to prove the contrary, Miss R. found that this was actually the case.)

Vespers over, Miss R. returned to her apartment

and made herself beautiful in a new 'dinner-suit,' preparatory to the arrival of a beau who took her to supper in an amusing restaurant and so completed a perfect weekend.

CHAPTER ELEVEN

YOU'D BETTER
SKIP THIS ONE

Now that we've had our say about extravagance, we are going to right-about-face. Probably, you had better not read this chapter at all. It's about *Saving*, that drab and old-fashioned virtue that has never been really enjoyed by anyone except the very penurious and Mr. Coolidge.

Most people, during the first thirty-odd years of their lives, are annoyed by anyone who talks in favor of saving. After that, they are even more annoyed to find that all that the Mr. Scrooges said was true. One of the gloomiest Facts of Life is that the most tiresome adages about a penny saved turn out to have something in them after all.

We are not advising you to save for any good and moral reason, but merely because, as time goes on, spending your own money has a kick in it, like whisky, while having other people's money spent on you has, at best, the tame pleasure of a glass of lemonade. It is at least twice as much fun to buy something at the ten-cent store with money that is yours and nobody else's, than to have enough money doled out to cover a purchase at Cartier's. And a good-sized majority of the women living alone have to do some saving if they're going to have this kick in the bitter end.

No girl in her teens believes this. Few girls in their twenties do. Lots of women in the thirties and forties haven't learned it. Almost all women are born with a belief that some man will marry and support them, or, at the worst, that a relative will die and leave them a fortune. This is probably an instinct implanted by Providence and has something to do with the propagation of the race. We haven't time to figure out just what, but there it is, and it takes a long, long time to uproot it.

But eventually, if no husband has turned up and no obliging relative has died, there comes a horrid conviction that putting aside a little something for a rainy day is not such a bad idea. And as time goes on, the rainy day looms up more and more as something inevitable and not something fictitious.

In the twenties, too, there is a notion that our wants get less as time goes on. But at the ripe old age of, say forty-two or -three, this turns out to be another delusion. Not only do you like expensive perfumes as well as ever; they are now a habit. By this time, you know more about good clothes, exotic foods, foreign cities, and other luxuries, and your tastes are more expensive accordingly. (We ourselves hate to think what we will cost at eighty.) The lady who does her economizing at the beginning of her life is the fortunate one. Fortunate, rather than wise, as this is almost always purely a matter of circumstance.

Then, too, living alone may be a tragedy at first, and a lonely business for several years, but eventually it may become a passion. For grim horror, just pause a minute and think about the woman who has lived charmingly in her own establishment for ten or twenty years and then had to move in as a dependent with some portion of her family. (And maybe not too congenial a portion.)

You might as well face the fact early in the game that if, at forty, you are living alone, you will probably still be living alone, or wishing you could, at fifty, sixty, seventy, and even eighty. Some of that time, at least, you will not be able to go out and earn your own Martinis. Once that gruesome fact is lodged in your mind, it may seem less desirable to spend all of your income the week before you get it.

If you have a flair for investments or are naturally thrifty, you may not need our words of wisdom. But if you belong to the much greater number of those who regard money as something to spend and who can make any stock go down by putting a little cash into it, or who look upon putting something in the savings-bank as a thing to be done week after next — you'd better read on.

Not for you are the enticing get-rich-quick schemes sold by persuasive young men. Not for you, even, are the milder forms of speculation urged by second cousins and old friends of the family. For you, there are only the trust funds, annuities, and other safe investments, which plod along their slow and sober ways, never making you rich, but eventually making you secure.

Once you have signed your name to a paper committing you to pay for one of these, you are in for it — which is as it should be. Ever so often, you have to pay, or lose at least part of what you've already put in, and so you pay, with the tepid comfort that, thirty years or so from now, when someone mentions the Old Ladies' Home to you, you can tell him what you think of him.

And what, you are probably thinking, about all the people who saved so piously and lost their money even then? We know all about bank failures, too, but we still think the good old system is a sounder one than any new one you may have thought up. If you put your money in the bank, the chances are at least ten to one that it will be there when you've saved enough to think about investments. If you've spent it, there isn't any chance at all.

When it comes to investing, in general, it's a good idea for the average, none-too-businesslike woman not to do it with relatives or even old friends. In the main, not even the most reliable individual is as safe as a good, substantial, well-known institution. Uncle Henry may be absolutely honest, but he may also slip behind the times, as years go on, or even get softening of the brain, which is scarcely likely to happen to a whole savings-bank or an insurance company. Talk to your brothers-in-law and old family lawyers and friends if you must, but at least talk to several of them.

We don't know why you must, as a matter of fact. You are probably lazy about money matters, like most of us, or perhaps you think that helplessness is appealing. Or you really share the widespread notion that finance is something that only the masculine mind can master. The result of that little idea is that even the most intelligent woman will ask business advice of a man who is scarcely bright rather than use her own judgment. The fact that he's never done anything very startling with his own investments doesn't matter at all. To the majority of women, the world of finance is as mysterious as the interior of the University Club and beyond her comprehension.

As a matter of fact, this is a world in which an increasing number of women are making successes. But even you and I don't need to have a gift, like a talent for music, in order to understand the simpler facts about finance. If we did, there would be an even greater rate of unemployment among the men we know. With a little reading, however – the financial section of a good daily paper or the literature of a few good financial institutions – we could probably learn enough to build up as good a background as the next man. We certainly could if we applied the same common sense to our investing that we do to our spending.

We know of one woman who was cleaned up neatly in a bank failure and who now checks the advice of her bank with that of three others in three other cities before she makes a move. We don't say that she's going to be rich, since this is the age when nobody knows what will happen next, but it wouldn't surprise us to see her buy back the family jewels.

When it comes to putting aside the necessary money, probably the surest means is the budget system, dull though it sounds (and is, to be honest). Not a hard-and-fast budget, with every stamp accounted for, but a flexible system that divides your income approximately. Don't follow anyone else's figures. Make your own, based on your own pet economies and extravagances. If you can afford a five-room apartment, but would rather manage with a two-room one and take a trip every year, take your trip. If you'd rather wear inexpensive clothes and go to the theater often, or expensive clothes and live on plain and simple food, go ahead. Don't worry if your scheme doesn't fit any of the books that tell what proportion of your income should go for what. After all, that's your business and not the author's.

The idea is to know where you are and where you will come out at the end of the year or month. This means planning at least in a general way for a good six months ahead, so that you won't think you're rich enough one month to buy a fur coat and then find out the next that you needed the money to pay the taxes. And however you budget, have one of your items marked, grimly, 'Savings.' This is not the same item as the one that pays for doctors' and dentists' bills and other catastrophes. You can call that 'Miscellaneous,' or 'Extras,' or 'Illness,' or any name that pleases your fancy. It may seem superfluous to you, occasionally it may even be superfluous, but, in that case, you can always blow it in on an evening coat or a trip to Bermuda.

CASES

Case XXVI: Miss Y. – Miss Y. hates figures just as much as you do. But Miss Y. sells underwear in a not too smart emporium, and she has discovered that the wages of selling are small. When on several occasions she found herself without lunch money for the last two days before pay-day, and then had to turn down a young man's invitation because she couldn't pay for a shampoo and her hair looked Too Awful, she resigned herself to a budget, which she follows at least in a general way.

Miss Y.'s salary totals $100 a month, and here is her system:

Home Sweet Home	$30.00
Breakfasts (good enough)	5.00
Lunches (pretty sketchy)	9.00
Dinners (good)	18.00
Wardrobe (this takes some doing)	15.00
Nuisances (light, ice, laundry, household supplies)	10.00
Fun (except when it goes to the dentist)	8.00
Saving	5.00
	$100.00

Now and then, Miss Y. borrows from Fun to pay for Nuisances, but she pays back at least approximately, and she no longer goes without lunch.

Case XXVII: Miss I. — Miss I. writes copy for an advertising agency and knows all about caviar and the new plays. But if you think that her financial problems are less crucial than Miss Y.'s, we are surprised at your lack of worldly wisdom. When Miss I. has had a ten-dollar-a-week raise, her scale of living has gone up fifteen dollars a week, and if she doesn't stick to the budget that her best friend has just worked out for her, we hate to think what Miss I. is coming to.

Miss I.'s salary is $50 a week or about $215 a month, and here is her budget:

Two-room apartment	$60.00
Breakfasts (and not just toast and coffee)	8.00
Luncheon (simple when alone; grand when with someone) . .	18.00
Dinners (at home and with style)	25.00
Clothes (here is the pinch)	30.00
Painful necessities (light, telephone, laundry, cleaner)	24.00
Indulgencies (theaters, hairdresser, entertaining)	25.00
Saving	25.00
	$215.00

This is what Mrs. H. (Miss I.'s friend) assures Miss I. can be done, and she knows what she's talking about. But we doubt if Miss I. will do it, as she is a lady who will try anything that looks like a bargain, can think of a reason why every day is a special occasion for celebrating, and always believes she's going to win the next sweepstakes.

Case XXVIII: Mrs. H. – Mrs. H. lives so charmingly that her friends think she lives extravagantly, but Mrs. H. earns, not fifty, but forty dollars a week. Now and then, she has a buffet-supper party with guests who like to come to her two-room apartment far more than they like to go to Park Avenue splurges. And the apartment is far more attractive than Miss I.'s, just as Mrs. H. is better dressed and better groomed.

The explanation is that Mrs. H. has a flair – not so much for making money as for making money go a long way. She knows that the greatest single economy is good taste, since it prevents you from making mistakes in spending.

Mrs. H.'s two-room apartment costs ten dollars a month less than Miss I.'s, and, before she moved in, the difference looked much greater than that. Now, the difference would seem to be the other way around. The rooms are as large and are painted a soft yellow-cream and the curtains are a flattering apple-green. Against this background, masses of laurel and huckleberry leaves in green glass vases (from bargain basements) look even more effective than the bowls of roses in which Miss I. indulges. The leaves last several weeks and have been known to last for months, while the roses, usually bought on the street, are thrown out the second day.

Mrs. H. has discovered that her friends enjoy her buffet suppers as much as a formal dinner (which she isn't equipped to give, even if she could afford it). She serves spaghetti and cheese, baked beans, diced ham and eggs baked in cream sauce; wooden bowls of chicory, romaine, escarole, and radishes with an epicurian French dressing, which she makes herself. Swedish bread, cheese (a tray of mixed varieties), and coffee complete this meal and you wouldn't believe it if we told you how little it costs.

Mrs. H. budgets so successfully that she has enough money ahead to take advantages of sales, but she never buys more of anything – from clothes to dish-towels – than she needs to keep going comfortably, having learned that the more you have, the more time and service it takes to keep things up. Mrs. H. keeps what she has up to top-notch.

Case XXIX: Miss O. – Miss O., at fifty-eight, has retired after a long career with a publishing firm. She is living in a charming small house in a suburb of Chicago, with a garden and a garage. She bought the house with the money which she put, in small amounts, in a Home Building and Loan Company, for every week of well over twenty years. As this was the bulk of her savings, Miss O. owns very little in addition to her house, but the house has three large master bedrooms, as well as a maid's room. Miss O. occupies one room herself and rents another to a widowed school friend. The third is occupied by two sisters, slightly younger than Miss O., who still go to business. This pays for a maid and gives Miss O. a small income.

All of The Girls, as they are known to their friends, have lived hard-working and uneventful lives by themselves until they joined forces. Now, however, they are having their fling. Each has a hobby. Miss O.'s is gardening, the widow's is motoring, and the sisters go in for painting and genealogy, respectively. They drive about the country on week-ends and holidays, entertain at dinner and bridge, and have learned to shake their own cocktails.

Case XXX: Miss Van D. – The sad story of Miss Van D. is due to the fact that she was a Beauty. Blonde, slender, and willowy from the age of fourteen, everybody, including her parents and herself, believed that Miss Van D. would be a heartbreaker, but, by eighteen, her ideas of a good marriage had become so inflated that none of her suitors were good enough.

When Miss Van D.'s parents died and she found herself with very little money, she was still blonde and willowy, and still hopeful. She came to New York, where she felt that there were more people capable of appreciating her pink-and-white charm. She had little difficulty in finding a position as a model – but this was not very profitable nor did it prove to be a road to matrimony. Miss Van D.'s slim figure showed off gowns and wraps to the greatest possible advantage, but usually to wealthy matrons and stout dowagers, all fiction about beautiful models to the contrary.

Miss Van D. acquired some admirers, but those who were sufficiently rich had intentions other than matrimony, and vice versa. She felt that it was only sensible to spend her last penny on clothes, hair, and skin, her personal appearance being her chief asset. As time went on, this began to cost more and more, and the suitors began to grow fewer and fewer. Miss Van D.'s standard of a good marriage shrank, too, with time, but her opportunities never quite caught up with it.

Eventually, Miss Van D. had to change her occupation from modeling to clerking in a bookstore. By this time her beauty was a trifle artificial and

faded. Masculine book-lovers were more numerous than masculine shoppers for ladies' clothes, but most of them were poor.

Miss Van D. is still clerking in the bookstore, but she is no longer a beauty, and she sometimes wakes up in the night wondering what happens to people when they no longer have a job and have no money in the bank.

CHAPTER TWELVE

MORE ETIQUETTE FOR AN EXTRA WOMAN

QUESTION: Is it correct for a woman to go into a bar and have a cocktail, if she is alone in a city?

Answer: It is not incorrect for a woman to go alone into any bar that she can get into (some bars are for men only), but we don't advise it. In the first place, if you must have your drink, you can have it in a lounge or a restaurant, where you won't look forlorn or conspicuous, as you might in the bar. But in spite of our pæans to liquor, we are not for drinking alone. It's a gloomy truth that this is one of those things that turn out just as the Sunday-school books said. It gets to be a habit, and, while it may seem to be harmless while you are twenty- or thirty-odd, some day the goblins will get you. It's a wise lady who knows enough to confine her drinking to social occasions.

Question: If a woman is invited to a party at which she knows there will be men, but no mention is made of an escort, may she bring a man with her?

Answer: It depends on the party. If it's one for which an exact number of guests are planned – a luncheon, a dinner, an evening of bridge, a theater party, or any occasion where conveyances will be needed – certainly not. Your hostess has undoubtedly provided a man for you, and he may prove more interesting than the one you planned to take. Or he may not, but you'll have to make him do, anyway.

If it's a larger party – a small dance, a cocktail party, or a buffet supper, for instance, you might call up your hostess and ask if you may bring a guest with you. She'll probably be grateful.

If it's an enormous reception or dance, just take your man along. No one will be the wiser – your hostess least of all.

If you're the type that must always have an escort, whatever the party, you can, after all, stay at home.

Question: When a lady lives alone with one servant, in a five-room apartment in a suburb of New York, how much service may she expect from the maid?

Answer: She may expect the maid to do everything – except, perhaps, clean the windows and wash the sheets and bath-towels. If she's a really smart woman, she will look upon her maid very much as a bachelor looks upon his man – and get much the same results. We know of one business woman – also living in a suburb – who has acted on this principle for many years, and, though she is far from domestic, whose ménage is the envy of her married friends. Her maid not only cooks, cleans, and washes, she also mends and presses her mistress's clothes, does the marketing, and drives the car. She meets trains morning and night and does innumerable errands, all with neatness, dispatch, and an enthusiasm based on the fact that her mistress looks upon her as another woman with a job, and gives the same consideration to her free time as would be given in an office.

During the three years which this particular maid has had the position, she has greatly increased her own value by learning to run a car as well as a vacuum sweeper; grasping the fine points about serving breakfast on a tray; getting to know just what ingredients to have ready for practically any type of cocktail; and overcoming the passion that most maids feel for dabs of whipped cream.

Question: With all the terrible things one reads in the paper, is there any way that a woman can be really safe living alone in a large city?

Answer: Nobody is entirely safe anywhere, alone or not, but the type of thing to which you refer is no more likely to happen to a woman living alone than to anyone else. We don't know why, but offhand, we can't think of a single good murder case with a woman who lived by herself as the victim. We can, of course, think up a lot of good reasons why terrible things could happen to her in her unprotected state more easily than to a woman living with her husband and thirteen children. We can also think of reasons why you are more likely to be killed flying than traveling by train, and vice versa; motoring than walking, or the other way round; or coming downstairs than skating in the park.

However you live, your chances of having anything spectacularly terrible happen to you are one out of several hundred thousand. Your chances of winning in a sweepstakes are a lot better. But have you ever won one?

Question: May a woman traveling alone talk to men who are fellow travelers without being introduced – especially on shipboard?

Answer: If you are old enough to travel on shipboard alone, you are old enough to talk to anyone who interests you. This is, in fact, the perfect place to do a little experimenting. You may have some odd experiences, but you will be a broader woman accordingly. An ocean trip has the special advantage of being quite separate from the rest of your life. Friends you make on the ship, you need

never see again if you don't want to. Moreover, you can proceed without the eyes of family or friends upon you. Often you can have a delightful time with someone you would be embarrassed to know at home. At the same time, you needn't bother with some bore who would probably be in the same set in your home town. Contrary to all your early instructions, it's a good idea to start any trip with an open mind and speak when spoken to – till you find out that you'd rather not pursue the conversation. This was once considered a Grave Danger, but any modern girl knows how to meet it. If she doesn't, there's always the conductor or the captain.

This general attitude, not too literally followed, is not a bad one to take through life. If you do so, you will probably not have to live alone and like it.

THE END